Seven Crossroads of Night

SEVEN CROSSROADS OF NIGHT: QUIMBANDA IN THEORY AND PRACTICE
Copyright © 2023 Nicholaj de Mattos Frisvold
Cover image 'Exu Ferro' by Luciana Lupe Vasconcelos.
Pontos riscados illustrated by S. Aldarnay.
All Rights Reserved.

ISBN 978-1-914166-13-6 (Hardcover)
ISBN 978-1-914166-14-3 (Paperback)
ISBN 978-1-914166-16-7 (Ebook)

A catalogue for this title is available from the British Library.
10 9 8 7 6 5 4 3 2 1

Except in the case of quotations embedded in critical articles or reviews, no part of this book may be reproduced or transmitted in any form or by any means, electronic or mechanical, including photocopying, recording, or by any information storage and retrieval system, without permission in writing from the publisher.

Nicholaj de Mattos Frisvold has asserted his moral right to be identified as the author of this work.

Hardcover edition printed by Biddles, Norfolk.

First published in 2023
Hadean Press
West Yorkshire
England

www.hadeanpress.com

Seven Crossroads of Night

Quimbanda in Theory and Practice

Nicholaj de Mattos Frisvold

Acknowledgments

There are many who deserve gratitude and recognition for having been part of the journey that led to the manifestation of *Seven Crossroads of Night*; amongst the named and nameless I want to express my gratitude to Katy, steady partner in life and love for twenty-one years, and to all the sons and daughters of our Cabula/temple Meia-Noite da Encruzilhada. I want to thank my consistent and wise spirits that have followed me for the last two decades, Exu Morcego, Exu Meia-Noite, Pomba Gira Cigana, and Pomba Gira Rainha das Sete Encruzilhadas. Likewise, great appreciation goes out to true brothers and friends, Aluísio and Diego de Oxóssi, and a big thank you and gratitude to Erze and Hadean Press for making this book possible and to Humberto for composing the preface.

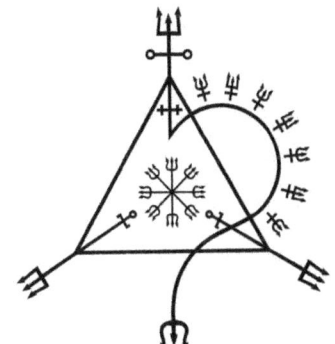

CABULA MEIA·NOITE DA ENCRUZILHADA

Contents

Exu Welcomes All by Humberto Maggi ... 1

Chapter 1: *The Origin of Quimbanda* ... 4

Chapter 2: *True Quimbanda* ... 17

Chapter 3: *On the 'Fundamento de Quimbanda'* ... 28

Chapter 4: *On Hierarchies* ... 38

Chapter 5: *The Syntax of Quimbanda* ... 45

Chapter 6: *Quimbanda Spirits* ... 53

Chapter 7: *On Possessions* ... 61

Chapter 8: *A Quimbanda Cosmology* ... 67

Chapter 9: *How to Understand Exu* ... 74

Chapter 10: *How to Understand Pomba Gira* ... 81

Chapter 11: *The Realm of Quimbanda* ... 88

Chapter 12: *The House of Exu* ... 96

Chapter 13: *Working Macumba* ... 105

Chapter 14: *To Bind Desire* ... 114

Chapter 15: *Murderous Sorcery* ... 120

Chapter 16: *Works for Gain and Money* ... 129

Chapter 17: *The Fat Evil Eye* ... 135

Chapter 18: *Quimbanda and Healing* ... 140

Chapter 19: *Spirit Houses* ... 145

Chapter 20: *Living Quimbanda* ... 152

Chapter 21: *Calunga* ... 158

Appendix I: *Approaching the Entity* ... 163

Appendix II: *The Kingdoms of Quimbanda* ... 187

Bibliography ... 195

Index ... 197

Exu Welcomes All

There is a veil that separates the worlds; everywhere and from the beginning, a traffic of influences and offerings has been established between the flesh and the spirit. What exists on the other side remains elusive, and is identified by sensitives through the body: communication takes place through the vibration that runs through us and is (de)coded by the mind in a simulacrum of the senses. Different emotions react to this communion, as our mind and our body react to the presence of other spirits.

Different theologies place different values on this experience; energies, colors and shapes can be accepted or rejected by the religious discourse. The Christian West favors blue and white, and the celestial sphere; the rejected and the condemned of the Church were given the colors black and red, and were destined for the underground world. These symbolic prejudices from the era of slave colonialism onwards were extended over the violated races and cultures.

In colonial Brazil, a brotherhood of the needy was established through pact, between the Portuguese exiled by the Inquisition, the Africans enslaved by the Crown, and the invaded and deceived indigenous peoples. It is here that the hybrid trees take root, where in their grafts Quimbanda will later flourish, the magical art par excellence of those marginalized by the Church and the State. Quimbanda's marginalization is also established in a double way, as the entities whom it recognizes define themselves by archetypes and stereotypes that the 'good' society rejects. With its alliance between devils and dead people of 'bad reputation', sinful priests and prostitutes, gypsies and vagrants, witches and sorcerers, Quimbanda gathers the army of those rejected by Heaven and the city, by God and by His representatives on earth. Quimbanda is revolt and rebellion, even if the reaction comes a moment later, in a 'rasteira malandra'.

My approach to Quimbanda was not something planned; I often joke that just as goetia was meddling with Crowley, Quimbanda was meddling with me. To fall in love with Quimbanda I had to break down prejudices and open my eyes. Spontaneous experiences where Quimbanda 'meddled' with me were fundamental, but also very important was the work of Frisvold.

In 2012 Frisvold and Scarlet Imprint published *Exu & the Quimbanda of Night and Fire*, a year after *Pomba Gira and the Quimbanda of Mbumba Nzila*; these two works mark a historic moment, in which Quimbanda as an object of culture receives an international exhibition and is raised to the same level of respect and visibility as traditions such as traditional European magic. Suddenly, Quimbanda is not just another practice limited to the Brazilian outskirts and suburbs, it is highlighted center-stage in the international esoteric demimonde, with its spirits cataloged in luxury editions for the English-speaking market, that is, worldwide.

These two works by Frisvold were very important in my approach to Quimbanda; they helped me to glimpse beyond the conditioned cultural bias that prevails in Brazil, where this art and craft is still seen with prejudice, both religious and class. For the Christian majority, it is clearly the Devil's Art, and, in fact, we don't deny it. It is seen as something that belongs to the poor and bad people—class prejudices often make these the same thing. That this class prejudice is at odds with the ethics of Christianity does not surprise us—it is yet another example of the hypocrisy necessary for anyone who wants to be rich and Christian at the same time.

Beyond this veil of religious and social mistakes, Frisvold's work opens us to the true essence of Quimbanda, where royalty and power, goodness and justice, meet under the banners of Exu and the Devil. While those who are unable to tear the veil debate whether or not Eshu is the Devil, in the astral wilderness where Quimbanda reigns we are initiated to see beyond these symbols inherited and syncretized from the heritages of Europe and Africa.

In this new work, Frisvold teaches us that to thread the path of Quimbanda, our bond with Exu must be "visceral and strong";

he talks about Quimbanda as a commitment for life, a pact to be honoured and respected to the grave—and beyond. This may bring to mind the superstitious ideas developed among Catholics about pacts with the Devil, but Quimbanda actually rescues the oldest practices of communion between man and spirit that Christianity has distorted. So here in this magnificent work we are reminded that "pact means a contract written in earth, blood and fire that establishes a lifelong bond between entity and man"—as it always was before and outside Christianity. Also, the *fundamento*, the foundation of the practice, is here explained in its multiple significations, and even deeper and more mysterious understandings are hinted at to the attentive reader. Frisvold navigates with elegance between practical advice, cosmological explanation and the description of the spirits.

Quimbanda began its flirtation with writing through the first Umbanda writers, like Leal de Souza and Lourenço Braga, who left few notes on a reality that they, however much they wanted to, could not deny. But the first author to give Quimbanda priority treatment was another Umbandista, Aluizio Fontenelle, in the early 1950s. Today, Frisvold is one of the essential authors who carry out the triple task of purifying Quimbanda from religious additions that do not understand its true essence, bringing the discourse on Quimbanda to a new level that reveals its true nobility, and spreading its fire throughout the world.

The spirits are grateful.

Humberto Maggi
Kingdom of Ndongo
MMXXI

CHAPTER ONE

The Origin of Quimbanda

Ele é o capitão da encruzilhada, ele é
He is the captain of the Crossroad, he is
Ele é ordenança de Ogum
He is given sole authority from Ogum
Sua coroa, quem lhe deu foi Oxalá
His crown was given to him by Oxalá
E seu tridente quem lhe deu foi Omulu
His trident was given to him by Omulu
Oi salve o Sol, salve a estrela, salve a Lua
Salutations Sun, salutations Star and Moon
Saravá Seu Tranca-Rua
We are saluting Tranca Rua
Bebendo marafo no meio da rua
Drinking booze in the middle of the street

Quimbanda is the name given to the cultivation of Exu and Pomba Gira, hence we find Quimbanda used as a word to define working with these spirits as much as their proper cults. Any attempt at finding the more true or most traditional house of Quimbanda is likely to fail because these ideas are embedded in the connection and pact each and every Tata and Yaya holds with their Exu and Pomba Gira.

Currently we have many ideas about where Quimbanda came from, and in truth it arose from various avenues and was filtered through countless crossroads; it might be more useful to think about Quimbanda as a fisherman's net covering the entirety of Brazil, and each node in the net representing a fragment of Quimbanda. It is difficult to define the exact moment when the word *Quimbanda* was first used, at least in written form, but what we can affirm is that Quimbanda as a word associated with the cult of Exu and black magic entered the vernacular with the 1942 publication of Lourenço Braga's bestseller *Umbanda, Magia Branca e Quimbanda, Magia Negra* in which Braga follows in the footsteps of the series of articles the Umbandist and journalist Leal de Souza wrote in 1932. In this series of articles, de Souza expanded upon his pioneering work from 1925 where he brought into print the 'lines of Umbanda', and wrote about what he called the African line or the line of *pretos-velhos*, Old Blacks, naming it *Linha de Santo*, the line of saints, that is typified by a 'father of the table' that has his 'head crossed'. To have the head crossed referred to someone who received *caboclos*, *pretos-velhos*, or Exu in possession. De Souza was clearly uncomfortable with the presence of this 'black line' in Umbanda and saw it as having the function of serving the 'white line', as the black line was largely composed of spirits that were primitive and wild, hence they had to be indoctrinated and trained. The way that was done was to treat these spirits as subservient to Orixás and Catholic saints. From this period onward Quimbanda gained the connotation it has today as a cult of black magic and diabolism presided over by Exu and Pomba Gira, and became more and more associated with being 'the left side' of Umbanda. Prior to this, the practice we know as Quimbanda and the work with diabolic spirits was referred to as 'macumba', a term used even to this day to describe 'black magic' in general and Quimbanda in particular. In order to give an elegant summary of these forces that generated what we today know as Quimbanda, Humberto Maggi in his erudite article 'The Gnosis of the Devil' writes the following:

> Brazil was the last country in the Western world to abolish slavery, in 1888. However, this late act of humanity was not followed by policies of integration and the great mass of ex-slaves was severally marginalized.
>
> In Rio de Janeiro the African descendants occupied a large area in the center of the city, where they mingled with European immigrants and other people ill-favored

by Fortune. This hotbed of prostitutes and capoeiras1 was the cradle of the syncretic magical-religious movement named Macumba.

It is very difficult to describe with accuracy the characteristics of the Macumba as it developed in the end of the XIX century, before its rituals were refurbished by the creators of the Umbanda in the first four decades of the XX century. We know that its main influence was from the Bantu religion, brought by the Congo-Angolan slaves who were majority in Rio de Janeiro. Bantu religion dealt deeply with the cult of the ancestors, seen as active forces with whom the living could interact. Many traces of Bantu religious practices are discernible in the Macumba...

...It is very difficult to determine when African or European traditions were more important in the development of a certain feature of Quimbanda, but at the moment I tend to think that the Bantu people provided the basic ritual performance, with the centrality of trance possession, and European demonological magic provided the aesthetic features like the images of the exus and pombagiras. The inception of European magical thinking into the structure of African rituals happened since the beginning of the slave traffic to Brazil.[2]

You have now an idea of the origins of Quimbanda and why it is impossible to define a single root for Quimbanda; it simply doesn't work that way. Also, as Maggi points out, slavery was not abolished until 1888, but prior to this, around 1830, there was a great shift in Brazil as the government prepared themselves for the end of slavery. 1850 was the year when the purchase and trade

---

1 Capoeira is a martial art created by the slaves in Brazil, mixing dance and acrobatics. The capoeiras of the 19th century were bands of adepts of this martial art who hired out their skills or committed small crimes.
2 In the anthology *Scientia Diabolicam*, Hell Fire Club Books, 2018.

of slaves was forbidden globally; this also affected Brazil which then had to rely on the existing workforce along with the children who had been born into slavery, effectively ending the reign of the slave owners. The decades from 1830 until 1920 were formative for Brazilian spirituality and culture in many ways. One of the preparations made by the Brazilian authorities was to open for mass immigration in an attempt to make Brazil more European and less African—Brazil was one of the countries with the biggest African populations amongst the colonies. We shall not go into the extent of the cruelty exercised upon slaves in Brazil; it should suffice to say that Brazil was so worried about the African population being so large that they arranged for immigration solely from European countries—and Japan. We should also add that in the years prior to the abolition in 1888, the Ministério da Fazenda, who kept all of the records of what happened in the agricultural sector of Brazil (including much anthropological and ethnographic research), burned the majority of their anthropological archives. Hence from these actions we can conclude that there was a real fear amongst Brazilian colonizers of repercussions arising from the African population.

The oldest *terreiro* of Candomblé in Brazil is called *Casa Branca do Engenho Velho* (*Ilê Axé Iá Nassô Ocá*). It was founded in 1830 in Salvador, Bahia, and marks the beginning of these looser domestic cults taking an organized shape in the urban environment so as to be more protected by the law. Brazil went through turbulence itself a few years before this in gaining its independence from Portugal in 1822. Not only this, but the stories of Dessalines and the slave revolts in Haiti, leading to the island's independence also inspired the slaves in Brazil, which saw an increase in slave revolts and uprisings in the same period. Hence it was decades of perpetual transformation, and the biggest one for our subject was the urbanization of Brazil, as seen in the example of the *terreiro Casa Branca*. From 1830 to 1860 several *terreiros* of Candomblé were registered, predominantly in Bahia, Rio de Janeiro, Minas Gerais and Maranhão. These *terreiros* were from different nations, and thus we find, for instance, Candomblé de jéjé, which preserves the memory from Abomey in Benin, better known as Vodou. We have Candomblé de Angola, Candomblé de Caboclo, Candomblé de Ijexa, and most widespread, Candomblé Ketu, which preserves the Yoruba legacy. Candomblé de Ketu exercised a dominant influence in the formative years of Candomblé, roughly from 1840 to 1910, due to the increase in travel to *Guiné* or Africa by freed slaves wanting to connect with their roots. In these decades Lagos was a melting pot of African culture and the Africans coming over tended to stay there to connect with their ancestry, which led to much of the traditional wisdom being reflected thorough Ketu or Yoruba lenses. In addition, from the 1830s the production of coffee and sugar was extremely high in Brazil and the plantations needed a labour force, leading to offers being made to Africans in Lagos, i.e. modern-day Nigeria, to come to Brazil as paid workers. This in turn led to the Yoruba assuming a different social role, coming over as free men and women—hired workers and not slaves.

We might say that in Candomblé, Brazilian spirituality went through a reform of its own, adjusting itself to a bigger audience and urban surroundings. Prior to 1830, when Candomblé was chosen to be the legal term for houses that cultivated their African legacy, there were several names given to African and Afro-derived practices, all words carrying associations with dance and music, such as *calundo, cabula, mina, macumba, batuque, batucajé* to mention a few. One account speaks of a Portuguese traveller, Marques Pereira, arriving to a farm in Bahia in 1728 where he is unable to sleep at night because the sound of songs and drums, which for him sounded like "a confusion from Hell", kept him awake. The owner of the farm the morning after told Pereira that this was the sound of the *calundus*, and that it was better to leave these celebrations and old ways from their homeland, which he said were of a divinatory nature, alone.[3] We have from the same century accounts of a famous sorcerer with the name Antônio Calundu in the state of Pernambuco. Amongst his magical arsenal he was said to dance in possession, to play the drums, to

---

3 Da Silva, 1994: p. 43, 44.

make readings by the use of cowry shells, prescribe herbal baths, and was working with "idols in stone and other materials", but also crucifixes and "angels". Salvador and Rio de Janeiro became important urban centres for Candomblé, and in the shadow of Candomblé followed the legacy of *calundus* and *cabulas* in Bahia, becoming houses of macumba in Rio de Janeiro. Since the early twentieth century, macumba has become the vernacular for sorcery and spell work; macumba, like *calundo* and *cabula*, is a word of Kikongo origin, revealing some sort of persistence in sorcery being of a Kongo/Angolan origin, but carrying the same ideas as the Kimbundu word *macumba*.

In the early days of Brazilian anthropology we find the anthropologist Nina Rodrigues and the psychiatrist Arthur Ramos standing out, and when we examine their studies we find that at this time, between 1901 and 1930, there was some struggle in understanding the diversity contained within the words being used. Candomblé and macumba were used interchangeably, and macumba, through the instrument of the same name of Angolan and Kongo origin, was probably over time given an association with Quimbanda due to the spiritual practices of the people from these districts sharing particular commonalities. One of these commonalities was that they didn't make a natural fit with the ketû Orixás, and were loosely referred to as 'the African line' or 'the line of souls'. This would suggest that macumba, or what we today generally call Quimbanda, was passed through a great number of *terreiros* as a 'sorcerous secret', which is why we today have forms of Quimbanda that leans towards Candomblé in various ways and others towards Umbanda. The psychiatrist and ethnographer Arthur Ramos in *O Negro Brasileiro*[4] suggests that every form of Candomblé and macumba was a result of some form of syncretism, and he presents six forms of syncretism taking shape in the following configuration:

---

4 1940, p. 127.

Jeje-nagô
Jeje-nagô-muslim
Jeje-nagô-bantu
Jeje-nagô-mulim-bantu-caboclo
Jeje-nagô-muslim-bantu-caboclo-spiritist
Jeje-nagô-muslim-bantu-caboclo-spiritist-catholic

Edison Carneiro, a pioneer in the study of the African roots of Brazilian expressions of faith, states in his book *Religiões Negras*:[5]

> The African cults did not arrive in a pure state from Africa. The trade of Africans since the fifteenth Century placed Africans and Europeans in direct contact with one another. Catholic Europeans, Protestant Europeans. In the populace itself (in Brazil) we found Natives, Muslims, Jews and a host of others. And so, the disorganized Luso-Brazilian slave trade brought together, in the same place, Africans from the most diverse provinces, which enabled a fusion of mythologies as new ones were erected and others were forgotten.

It might be in these observations from Carneiro and Ramos that we find the origin of the lines of Quimbanda that was developed by Leal de Souza already in 1925. In that year he had generated a proto-line where macumba and Spiritism merged with Candomblé influences as they were presenting the first lines of Umbanda. What is salient here is that the Yoruba spirits, the Orixás, are given an elevated position, while the Bantu, Angolan and Kongo heritage were crammed together in one line, the line of souls, the African line, that was in practice the line of Quimbanda.

The Line of Oxalá (Nosso Senhor do Bomfim)
The Line of Ogum (Saint George)
The Line of Euxoca (Oxossi) (Saint Sebastian)

---
5 1936, p. 94 (trans. by Nicholaj de Mattos Frisvold).

The Line of Xangô (Saint Jerome)
The Line of Nhan-San (Iyansan) (Saint Barbara)
The Line of Yemanjá (Our Lady of Conception)
The Line of Almas (Souls, the African Line of Saint Cyprian)

In the following decade the lines changed—and so did their content. We find the Line of Oxalá turning completely Catholic, not only venerating the legions of saints like Anthony, Rita, Catherine and Expedite, but also departed Africans who during their life were good Catholics. The Line of Yemanjá turns into a line of multiple legions where we find sirens, undines, and *caboclos* of waters, mythological creatures like the freshwater dolphin, boto, and the riverine nymph Yara. This line also hold a particular affinity with Mary Magdalena, Venus, the Moon and Polaris. The Line of Iyansan is substituted with the Line of the Orient, seen as being commanded by Joseph of Arimathea, and here we find nearly all kinds of people venerated, from Eskimos to Europeans, Japanese to Arabians. The Line of Oxossi and Xangô was filled with Indian spirits and *caboclos*, while the Ogum were considered guardians of peoples like the Malei, the Nagô and given places in nature. Lastly the Line of Souls, defined as the African line, lost its saint and was seen as being ruled by Father Cabinda, in reference to the slave port in the Kongo delta. Here, in Cabinda, we find legions of Angola, Guiné, Kongo, Mozambique and so forth, all with their Masters and Fathers.

It is in this climate that Quimbanda takes shape—like in a mirror darkly it shows its resistance; with wings, claws, and African blood it rises within seven lines, which were detailed in the mid-1930s. We shall look at these lines within the African line in more detail and allow some speculation as to what these forms of Quimbanda might have viewed as central for their macumba.

The first line was the Line of Souls ruled by Omolu and his legions of cemetery ghosts and ghouls. To this line was ascribed everything African and in particular the *pretos-velhos*, or 'old blacks', that were considered to be repositories of magical knowledge. Omolu or Obaluwaye was the Orixá that was assigned to this line. Omolu was syncretized with St. Lazarus, and prior to that with St. Cyprian, and hence Omolu as the Lord of Death was highlighted through St. Lazarus, and the antinomian, magical and heretical qualities by St. Cyprian. We might guess that this form of macumba or Quimbanda held *pretos velhos quimbandeiros* as central, together with the legacy left by St. Cyprian in his many grimoires popular both in Iberia and in Brazil.

The Line of Skeletons of the Cemetery ruled by João Caveira (John Skull) and his legion of hungry ghosts followed naturally in sequence of importance, as in this line the focus was on the departed souls as guides and entities of work and communion. We might suggest that this form of macumba was very direct, with an intense focus on the many mysteries of the cemetery which today are embedded in a host of Exus and Pomba Giras, like Exu Caveira, Exu Asa Negra, Exu Morcego, Exu Meia-Noite, Pomba Gira da Calunga, Pomba Gira Maria Quiteria, and others.

The third line was called Nagô or 'Quimbanda de raiz' and was ruled by Exu Gererê, a marine Exu, and given dominion over the crossroads. This form of Quimbanda that borrows elements from Candomblé, especially Candomblé de Angola, is perhaps the form most widespread as this Quimbanda is the one that was more often passed through the *terreiros* of Bahia and Rio de Janeiro. I would say that any Quimbanda using *padê* in their work with Exu do have some ties to this form of Quimbanda. We can also see that this style of Quimbanda may or may not resort to Orixás, in particular Ogum, but as with all styles of Quimbanda every house of macumba is in perpetual flux and transformation as they move in unison with the cosmic pulse and the rhythm of the world.

The fourth and fifth lines are interesting as here we find a lot of overlays and overlapping. The fourth is the Mossorubi or Muslim line, ruled by Exu Kaminaloá, viewed as a volatile and primitive Exu, often cannibalistic in features, but equally often as a convert to Islam. The fifth line is the Malei line and is presided over by Exu Rei and Exu Marabô, with their legions of vicious and dangerous spirits of aristocratic and decadent leanings that know deep and dangerous secrets of the world, like how to control kiumbas (low astral entities or larvae). What is interesting here is that clearly in Exu Marabô we do find the memory of the Muslim *marabout*, a Muslim sorcerer, or Sufi wizard, as you wish. At the same time, Malei must be an etymological remembrance of the Malé people that caused a significant slave revolt in 1835, and was also the name given to a segment of white-dressed Ifá priests in Rio de Janeiro in the early twentieth Century. The Malé were Muslim Babalawos that were throwing opele and working both Ifá and Muslim sorcery to aid their clients. In spite of this crossover that doesn't make much sense at first, the most essential part of the cult of Quimbanda Malei is the use of stones, which would suggest that the Malei Quimbanda do connect to the Malé by a transition of the Esu stone, so central in Ifá, into the most central part of the practice. Likewise, the reputation of the Malé was fierce; yes, they dressed in white and displayed good character, but they also knew the darkest of all forms of magic, which is the reputation of the Malei line even today. The sixth line is the Line of *Caboclos Quimbandeiros* ruled by Pantera Negra (Black Panther) and his legions of savage spirits, both African and Indian, that connects to the legacy of the land itself.

Lastly there is the mixed line ruled by Exu Campinas (Exu of the plains) and his myriad hostile spirits, which has come to denote any form of Quimbanda not really fitting in the other lines or styles. Of interest is the fact that this is so very characteristic of Quimbanda, if not Brazilian spirituality at large; there is always room for what *is*, even if it is not fully understood, or where it belongs is not obvious. So just like Leal de Souza made a line for everything African that did not fit very well with the Orixás, so we see that even given an Orixá, like Omolu, the seventh line will always be an ambiguous realm of what belongs but is not so easily defined.

Another element is that each Exu and Pomba Gira is seen by Umbandists as having roads of their own. This means that there is an Exu Caveira of the Souls, just as there is an Exu Caveira of the Crossroad and so on. This manifold segmentation is there in order to give added quality and direction to the potency being worked with, and this touches upon how a given power works differently in the many kingdoms. The power of Exu Caveira in his natural habitat, the Cemetery, will be different from this force found at the shores of the ocean.

Another scheme for organizing the spirits of Quimbanda is in terms of kingdoms. The kingdoms are as follows: Encruzilhadas (Crossroads), Cruzeiro (a reference to the big votary Cross in the middle of the cemetery), Mata Fields/Weeds), Calunga (Cemetery), Almas (Souls), Liras (Lyre) and Praia (Beach). This classification will be used in the spirit catalogue in this book. The kingdoms also present the Exus and Pomba Giras in their original station, as guardian spirits of specific portals in nature and places of power. In the kingdoms we meet original powers, whilst in the lines we meet teaching spirits. To have a good understanding of the kingdoms is most useful, because no work is being done unless licence is granted from the kingdom we work with. Exus from other lines and kingdoms can then enter as parts of the spirit host when a particular work is done, depending on what kind of work is done in the particular kingdom. Just like an army distributes its soldiers and commanders depending on the type of expedition being made, so it is with the spirit hosts established in kingdoms, workings and in life. These positions will not necessarily be the same as their rank in the hierarchy, but rather mediated by the temperament of the Tata and the *terreiro*.

Let us take one example—in the *ponto cantado* at the beginning of this chapter we read: *"He is given sole authority from Ogum / His crown was given to him by Oxalá / His trident was given to him by Omulu."* We might interpret this *ponto* as suggesting that Exu is his own mystery, as Oxalá gave Exu the crown. As we saw, it was Omolu that was eventually assigned the role as overseer of this mystery, but the authority came from Ogum, and there is a long-standing connection between Exu and Ogum that up to just 1990 was very strong, so strong that Ogum was considered the doorkeeper of Quimbanda and each line was protected by a given Ogum, like in this listing that gives an example of how to distribute types of Ogum related to Quimbanda:

THE ORIGIN OF QUIMBANDA

Manifestations of Ogum in the Lines of Quimbanda

Ogum Malê	Line of Malei
Ogum Megê	Line of the Cemetery
Ogum Xoroquê	Line of the Caboclos Quimbandeiros
Ogum Rompe Mato	Line of the Mossorubi
Ogum Naruê	Line of the Souls
Ogum Beira Mar	Line Mista
Ogum Nagô	Line Nagô

This is just one example, as in other listings you find Ogum Megê listed two or three times since he is associated with the iron gate of the cemetery, and thus he is pivotal for access to the skeletons and the souls.

In closing this chapter, it is worthy to present some observations by Tata Oscar Ribas from his book *Ilundo* published in 1958, as during the 50s Quimbanda became associated with Umbanda, as the 'left hand' of Umbanda. Ribas imparts to us that in the Bantu culture, 'Quimbanda' was the name given to the diviner, exorcist, healer, and necromancer of the tribe. The function of the Quimbanda was to make diagnostics of different types, to re-establish harmony where there was friction, to annihilate the effects of negative workings, and in his repertoire as necromancer he also knew how to provoke death and misfortune. The Quimbanda was intimately connected to nature as he needed to make 'pacts' with spirits inhabiting places of power in nature and benefit from their guidance, and this also involved making bonds with plants and trees so he could use their natural power for medicine and venom. Ribas continues with a certain lament that as the negative reflex of Umbanda, the Quimbanda became just a sorcerer. He adds that becoming a Quimbanda can happen through three modalities, independent of Umbanda. He calls these three modalities spontaneity, transmission of the soul, and the intervention of the spirit guides.

The first modality is signified by tutorship under a master (Tata or Yaya) who during the various works and processes gives bits and pieces of the mysteries until the form is completed, and this is then sealed by ingesting secret powders that set ablaze the powers harvested over the years. Transmission of the soul refers to oneiric transmission where one is taken to the secret habitat of the masters, the 'kingdom' as it is called. The last modality is when the spirit guide, the Tata Exu or Yaya Pomba Gira, intervenes directly in dreams or in possession and performs the secret acts that make a Quimbanda.

All these elements must be present in contemporary Quimbanda as well, and the forest is of utmost importance as it is here in the forest that the spirits we nowadays call 'Exu' manifested for the first time as points of powers, the guides of sacred places the Bantu Quimbanda had to make pacts with in order to harvest the power he was searching for. This connection would then lead to a gradual awakening of the Quimbanda through dreams and tutorship. So how can we know if our Quimbanda is True Quimbanda? Let us explore this in the next chapter.

Chapter Two
True Quimbanda

Comigo ninguém pode
Nobody can match me
E nem há de poder
Nobody will have the strength
Minha banda é mais forte
My squad is the most powerful one
Que a banda de você
This is your squad
Saravá Umbanda, saravá Quimbanda
Hail Umbanda, Hail Quimbanda
Saravá quem manda, saravá você
Hail to who sends forth, Hail to you

Contemporary Quimbanda comes in many shades and variations, all of them being preserved either as a solitary domestic succession of macumba, in the sense of black magic worked with the aid of Tatas, *guias* or Exus, or passed on in some way or another in the shade of Candomblé or Umbanda. This means that the hunt for the original Quimbanda, where it all started, is futile and meaningless, as true Quimbanda came from a great variety of roots. As I am writing these words, we have four varieties of Quimbanda that are most widespread, or at least most spoken of, which are Quimbanda Nagô, also called Quimbanda de Raiz, Quimbanda Malei, Luciferian Quimbanda, and Quimbanda de Cruzeiro e Almas, also known as 'Quimbanda gaúcha' or 'Quimbanda of the Southern Brazil'.

If we turn back the clock to 1904, however, we find a curious little book, *As Religiões no Rio*, penned by João do Rio (1881–1921), a hedonistic dandy who at twenty-nine years old was elected to occupy a seat in the Brazilian Academy of Letters. In this book, this Brazilian Oscar Wilde paints a very vivid picture of the many forms of macumba found in Rio de Janeiro as a shorthand for Afro-derived magical practices. Hence, we can see that macumba was done through different styles honouring specific legacies. In the 1940s the different forms of macumba were not so much about 'tribal legacy', but were more a matter of defining places, like in Rio de Janeiro the forms of macumba were given the generic term *'macumba carioca'*, while in São Paulo they were in the same general way referred to as *'macumba paulista'*.

Macumba, however, was complicated from the perspective of law, regarded as a practice offending common sense and the dignity of the citizens. Private and domestic celebrations of non-Catholic cults and faiths were allowed since 1824, but in the public sphere doing so could be, and was, punished. Actually, what we see from the vivid accounts of João do Rio is a thriving and beautiful underworld of macumba, writers, actors, scoundrels, and prostitutes gathering together due to the umbrella of punishment covering them all indiscriminately. Hence even if there were centres of Candomblé registering their legacy already from 1830, it was never without risk that you would present yourself as a *'macumbeiro'*; rather you would present yourself as someone 'of faith' or someone who 'had saints' to avoid provoking the social ideas of religious decency. A welcome solution to this predicament came in the shape of Umbanda.

Zélio Fernandino de Morais (1891–1975) was a Brazilian medium who in 1908 announced this new religion called Umbanda. The announcement came through Zélio being incorporated or possessed by a spirit called Caboclo das Sete Encruzilhadas that appeared during a session of Kardecist Spiritism and gave a different direction for spirit work that would be far more universal than Kardec's. The fact that it was a *caboclo* manifesting was anathema to the Spiritists, who solely consisted of people from the white upper class. Even if Zélio channelling a spirit of the land was shocking and provocative, the Spiritist ideal of charity and understanding played out in Zélio's favour to such an extent that in 1935 we find seven temples or *terreiros* of Umbanda in the larger district of Rio de Janeiro, and already in 1927 we find the Tenda de Pai Benedito in São Paulo. Umbanda continued the Christian ideals of charity and was for all purposes Catholic, hence it became more and more common to define yourself as Umbandist or Spiritist instead of the loaded term '*macumbeiro*'. Especially from around 1918 Umbanda grew fast and strong, but always with the houses of macumba close by, quiet in the shadows of Umbanda, until we see in 1940 that Umbanda and Quimbanda were presented as two sides of the same coin. These formative years of Umbanda do deserve some more attention in order for us to understand the trajectory of macumba becoming Quimbanda. For Zélio, Umbanda and Quimbanda were the same thing, just different types of work; almost like Umbanda focused on working the Sun, and Quimbanda was relegated to the mysteries of the Moon and night. A famous *ponto cantado* sung to the first *preto-velho* in Umbanda in the *terreiro* of Zélio would show us how he understood the complexity of Quimbanda:

> Dá licença Pai Antônio, que eu não vim lhe visitar. Eu estou muito doente, vim pra você me curar. Se a doença for feitiço, bula-lá em seu congá; se a doença for de Deus, Pai Antônio vai curar. Coitado de Pai Antônio, preto-velho curador, foi parar na detenção, por não ter um defensor. Pai Antônio é quimbanda, é curador; Pai Antônio é quimbanda, é curador; é pai de mesa, é rezador; é pai de mesa, é rezador.

In translation it goes like this:

> Forgive me, Father Anthony, for I didn't came to visit you. I am very ill; I came for you to heal me. If the illness is through magic nail it down in your shrine; if the illness is from God, Father Anthony will heal it. Poor Father Anthony, old-black healer, he was locked up, because no one stood up for him. Father Anthony is Quimbanda, is healer; Father Anthony is Quimbanda, is healer; is

Father of the Table, is man of prayer, is father of the table, is man of prayer.

Quite interestingly we see in this *ponto* that Pai Antônio is a *quimbanda*, a healer, that he comes from Guiné, like all the Old Blacks, and like many *macumbeiros* of African origin he got locked up because no one stood up for him. And if there is one thing Exu and Pomba Gira do, it is to stand up as protectors, hence the *ponto* do speak of a resonance between the roles Exu have and what *pretos-velhos* had. This connection is further attested in how Exu was born from the African line. The African line was first presided over by St. Cyprian, then it changed to St. Lazarus, St. Benedict, and even St. Anthony, until today it is presided over by the Orixá Omolu.

Clearly Zélio was preoccupied with everything finding its place in Umbanda, that it should represent the rich diversity of spirits and faiths in Brazil. In recent years Zélio's legacy has suffered some critique due to the Catholic orientation he gave to Umbanda which led to a perceived 'colonial bias' regarding the African legacy in Umbanda. This might be so, but it is also true that Zélio was intrigued and genuinely interested in preserving macumba and the African line in the best possible ways. Hence, we see amongst the spirit classes of Umbanda, *pretos-velhos* and *caboclos*, that we have Caboclos Quimbandeiros and Pretos-velhos Quimbandeiros, denoting their affinity with the cult of Exu through their capacity as healers and magicians.

Besides Umbanda, the legacy of macumba was also preserved through Candomblé. For instance, the famous Pai de Santo Jamil Rachid in São Paulo opened a *terreiro* of Umbanda in 1948. In just five years there were five more *terreiros* in São Paulo. Of interest in the case of Pai Jamil is that prior to opening his *terreiro* he was 'made' in Candomblé, more specifically the nation jéjé (Vodou from Benin) in Salvador, Bahia, that preserved the legacy of *cabulas* and *calundus*, which was essentially macumba under a different name. And here comes the wonderful Brazilian touch to this: he was in a temple of Vodou consecrated to Obaluwaye, which is a *ketû* (Yoruba) Orixá, and his godmother had an intense and personal relationship with her *cabocla*. An observation like this is of great importance for what it says of the spiritual climate in Brazil, because Pai Jamil's case is not a curious one, it is more the norm than the exception. Reading this, it should be possible to understand how intricate everything is in Brazil and how the idea of finding the singular true root of Quimbanda is not only a fool's errand, but one that it is missing the mark completely. The following *ponto* might illustrate this quite beautifully:

> Seu Zé Pilintra não teve pai
> *Mr. Zé Pelintra don't have father*
> Seu Zé Pilintra não teve mãe
> *Mr. Zé Pelintra don't have mother*
> Ele foi criado por Ogum Beira Mar
> *He was made by Ogum of the ocean shore*
> Na fé de Zambi e de todos os Orixás
> *By the Faith of Nzambi and all Orixás*

This *ponto* is interesting because Zé Pelintra is considered an Exu, but he is also a master in Catimbó and as such reflects the typical Brazilian spirituality as related to the universe of macumba and Quimbanda. He was made or created by Ogum, the Orixá of fire and blacksmithery, but this particular Ogum, Beira Mar, also has secret ties with Quimbanda through Caboclos Quimbandeiros. He creates Zé Pelintra through the faith of Nzambi, which is the Kikongo name for the creative principle or God, together with all these Yoruba deities we know as Orixás. It is like the *ponto* is teaching us about the very core of Zé Pelintra being an entity that is spiritually supported by the Brazilian diversity in its totality. Zé Pelintra is actually a great icon for understanding the essence of Quimbanda. Zé Pelintra appeared first in the sorcerous tradition Catimbó in the state of Pernambuco where he is considered one of the 'masters of the table'. At the same time we find him described as a dangerous street kid, a doctor of the poor and a lawyer defending those who have no defence. His stories are told through

Zé Pelintra Valentão, José Phelintra de Aguiar and José Gomes da Silva, who each typified the life cycle of Zé Pelintra in different ways. These themes always involve the attitude of the hustler or the street-smart and cunning person who finds his demise in defending someone defenceless, almost always a woman. Zé Pelintra is considered cunning in sorcery, a true master of all the arts, especially the amatory ones. Even looking after himself he always has an eye for justice and helping those who are helpless. For

instance, the photo above is of a street art painting in Lapa, Rio de Janeiro, where we have the story of Zé Pelintra do Lapa who was stabbed to death after rescuing a woman from being raped. The place he died holds a shrine and a few meters away from the shrine this painting is found as Zé Pelintra do Lapa, encapsulating the atmosphere of Quimbanda. Zé Pelintra manifests what we know as the archetypical 'Carioca Exu', learned, street-smart, a hustler and a healer, but always with the tricky side of seeking advantage. In this way Zé Pelintra embodied macumba at large and how it shaped the very soul of Quimbanda as it took form already early on in the 20th century.

In the icon of Zé Pelintra we have one important facet of Quimbanda, and we also find another one in Rio de Janeiro, a sorcerer by the name of Juca Rosa. Looking at what he did and how he was perceived we are able to understand exactly what type of person and practice constituted what was later known as Quimbanda.

Some of the fundamental traces of the macumba can already be discerned in the descriptions of the rituals practised in the final years of the nineteenth century by the most famous sorcerer of the time, a man of African descent named Juca Rosa. Juca Rosa was in his time one of the most looked-for sorcerer in Rio de Janeiro, and he rose to fame due to several legal prosecution he suffered in 1871 for various forms of fraud and extortions. He had an impressive list of followers and clients from the upper strata of society, especially women. Numerous facts came out during the investigation for the fraud prosecution, though Juca Rosa himself was not ashamed of his work nor his growing wealth or numerous lovers.

The first thing that calls attention in the descriptions of these rituals and practices is that the essential framework is really of Bantu origin: the pillar of Juca Rosa's work was possession by ancestral spirits, mainly by a spirit named 'Pai Quibombo' ('Father Quibombo'/Tata Quibombo). We can see here already the first stages of what would become in the Umbanda of the twentieth century the important class of spirits named Old Blacks, as they all carry the title of 'father'. As we read in the PhD dissertation *A História do Feiticeiro Juca Rosa* by Gabriela dos Reis Sampaio:

> The oldest of the attendants who went for a long time to these activities, knew what they were about to witness. There would be music, dance, a lot of food and drink. At a certain moment, Rosa would go into trance, when, as it was said, he would receive spirits in his body, or "talk to the spirits," and then he was transformed or began to act as Father Quibombo, and not as José Sebastião da Rosa. In that state he attended the people, as he was now gifted with a "supernatural" power, as it was told by his followers.[6]

The music of the meetings was usually played by four musicians, two of them playing a percussion instrument called 'macumba'. That important detail was the reason why Juca Rosa

---

6 2000, p. 86 (trans. by Nicholaj de Mattos Frisvold).

was also known in Rio de Janeiro as the 'Chief of the Macumbas'. That indicates that the name macumba, which would become the popular denomination for this kind of magical work, was in origin an appellation given by outsiders of the cult due to the use of the musical instrument. We are also aware that Juca Rosa was not the only sorcerer to work like that in Rio de Janeiro at the time, but he was considered to be the most powerful.

The description of some of the works made by Juca Rosa for his clients is also very telling. He used black and red clothes, he offered up sacrificial items, and also made animal sacrifices.

What we see from this little glimpse into the works of Juca Rosa reveals a very simple structure:

1. The Tata/tutelary spirit of the Quimbandeiro is invited in to do the work or endow the vessel with the powers of his Tata.
2. Rhythm is used to attract spirits; in this case the reco-reco and drums, and thus these sounds came to be associated with 'macumba' going on.
3. Spirit offerings, including blood, were performed.
4. Magic/healing/help was performed in this altered state of consciousness with a spirit tied to the practitioner's ancestors, be it by blood or by spiritual descent.

A Bantu structure further emphasizes the importance of the woods, because the Bantu-speaking Kongo people were tied in to the mysteries of wood and plants, and hence we might suggest that when we speak of things 'Bantu' we are speaking of what the Yoruba referred to as the realm of Osanyin, the Lord of the Woods, the doctor of spirits. This suggestion will be in harmony with the accounts of missionaries recounted by Arthur Ramos and Nina Rodriguez, that emphasize how all these *ngiras* of the *macumbeiros* were held in the woods, and how the practitioners were sent out into the woods to bring back their Tatas and invite them to take possession of the medium.

Naturally on such simple premises we see that the Tata becomes supreme in importance. It's the Tata of the practitioner that enables the 'son' to effectuate miracles and works. The second important element here is the woods, woods symbolizing the origin of all spirits, the womb of everything coming to consciousness. So in a way, we all can trace our origin back to the woods, and this is also true for the kingdoms of Quimbanda; be it the Lyre, Street, Crossroad or Cemetery, it all still holds the echo and whisper of the woods of beginning, real or as a metaphor, be it the forest of dead ones, the forest of troubled people, or what not. It is an important idea to latch onto.

So when we take a raw look at our subject matter we find that Quimbanda is actually not something that can ever be a religion, because it is a cult of wood, spirit and tutelary spirits that teach you and empower you to do things. It is a sorcerous cult. Hence what Zélio did was to give a place to this particular spiritual expression, but since it was so alien from the educated ways of *mesa branca*, it had to be relegated to another place, what came to be known as the left side of Umbanda. But as we see in the case of Juca Rosa, and if we follow the descriptions of Bishop Nery in the seventeenth century speaking of the practices occurring in Espírito Santo and Minas Gerais, we find similar things happening, but with one distinction: here we find the report of two tables being erected, one for the 'saints' and another for 'the spirits of woods and the dead'. This latter table, always placed on the left, was for offerings of cachaça and tobacco. This was the table for the teaching spirits. Hence, we see that even in these earlier expressions of Quimbanda, prior to gaining this name, there was a focus on the left side being related to ancestry and guidance, tobacco, and booze.

Knowing that these ritual customs were already recorded and thus most likely transmitted, it is more likely that Zélio adopted 'macumba' as the left side in honour of what he himself received. The fact that Zélio for several years kept this 'practice of the left' closed from Umbanda and open only for a select few would attest to a continuation of macumba/Quimbanda within Zélio's

Umbanda, and that it was not a product of Umbanda per se. I believe he made a rescue operation, and as the few people still alive that knew him say about this, Zélio found the *mesa branca* to be too tamed. He had himself been subject to healing from a *caboclo*, and thus this motivated him to embrace the totality of Brazilian spiritual manifestations, not knowing that he was creating the first Brazilian religion. And *caboclos*, what are they? Spirits of the land, mestizos bridging black, white, Oriental, European and Native into a Brazilian form. What were the *pretos-velhos* that Zélio admitted into Quimbanda as teaching spirits, if not the African legacy of Brazil.

It so follows that after one hundred years under the umbrella of Umbanda, Quimbanda is a complicated beast to separate from Umbanda's left side, but not really. Quimbanda is still about spirits of the wood and ancestry, death, and more woods. It doesn't have a Christian ethos or dogma behind it, but after living well with a few elected saints both here and in the Kongo and Angola, an inversion of poles takes place where we, through applying the Kongo world view to the legacy we still have, can make sense of what appears to be a bigger mess than what it is.

Hence, Quimbanda is a cult rooted in a Bantu/Angolan principle. And what is this principle? That everything that has power is *nkisi* (power manifested), be it saint, stone, herb, act or thought. The importance rests in communion and connection with spirits, because Quimbanda is about a unique reflection of this wealth of possibility rooted in spiritual and ancestral legacy. It is because of this we so often see in *pontos,* and when people speak of Quimbanda, the wording *nossa quimbanda* (Our Quimbanda) as a salutation to the Tata of the particular *cabula* or house, who takes on the position as a tutelary spirit of these mysteries and teaches what we need, from the base of who we are, and generates this particular mystery that each and every house of Quimbanda represents.

So, this means that in a course like this we need to understand that the teaching is coming from a precise and well-defined gathering of spirits, the legacy of the people making part of this 'nossa quimbanda' as it is embraced in a Kongo atmosphere and faith. As told, the Kongolese spiritual world view sees potential for spiritual power in everything, but in this we also need to be honest and true to our Tatas that teach us, because in this we realize legacy and can become legion.

It follows that we will not speak badly about modern factions of Quimbanda, no matter how Satanic or modern they might appear to be. This is because our character serves as a measure for what kind of spirits we invite in to teach us, and so a person bent on the killing of every person that wronged him will also attract such spirits that teach this particular way. Also, as we saw from the case of Juca Rosa, pointing fingers and calling out the charlatan is never far away when we are dealing with mysteries and forces like this, hence to have some standards, to strive towards being a better person, to be generous and kind, is always the best defence of any 'black magician' that does not want to invite in hostile and troublesome spirits. We are speaking of vinculums and directions, harmony and dissonance.

A *cabula* or temple of Quimbanda should be a place where character is tempered through understanding how to walk through fire, and using it without being consumed by it. Quimbanda is about working both hands from and within this earth-fire. Quimbanda is a call for solace in the woods as much as we seek teaching from the Crossroad and understand how to bend the Lyre to our need and bathe in the Calunga for release.

CHAPTER THREE
On the 'Fundamento de Quimbanda'

Oh! Salve Exu
Oh! Salutations Exu!
Salve o Rei da Encruzilhada
Salutations to the King of the Crossroad
Que sem Exu, não se pode fazer nada
'Cause without Exu you can't do anything
Tumba le-lê, tumba la-lá
Falling hither, Falling tither
Que sem Exu não se pode trabalhar
Who don't have Exu can't work (with him)

To possess 'fundamento', foundation, is what gives you the right to work Quimbanda, but the idea of *fundamento* is not as straightforward as many would like it to be. The idea of foundation refers in the first place to 'having Exu or Pomba Gira', in the sense of their *assentamento* or Spirit House. When this Spirit House is made, a pact is made and teachings are passed from the teacher to the novice who in this moment becomes the caretaker of the Exu or Pomba Gira that has been seated, and the novice is elevated through this responsibility as Tata or Yaya. This is certainly the more clean and irrefutable way of possessing *fundamento* in a materialist culture such as ours, but at the end it all boils down to 'having Exu', that the sorcery you do with your Exu or Pomba Gira works, hence a part of having *fundamento* is also about having a connection with a spirit as well as possessing the necessary knowledge and secrets of the cult. It follows from this that in Brazil we can hear references to people who 'have the hand' in the sense of managing to deal well with a spirit, that they were 'born in Hell', that they were 'pre-made in the *farofa*'[7] or 'born in the boiling palm-oil'.

When it comes to the *assentamento*, the physical Spirit House, these can be made in many different ways, although in terms of ingredients there are clearly some repeating items that seem to make the core of the Spirit House. These can range from simple vessels of terracotta, predominantly containing stones, horns, minerals and other items of flora and fauna, to small sealed up vases of terracotta or porcelain, to cauldrons of iron and copper sealed with earth and cowry shells, decorated with elaborate ironwork or statues of the Exu the *assentamento* is made for.

Yet, the *fundamento* goes deeper than this and points towards an indwelling power, that you are able to show in one way or the other that the bond between you and Exu is visceral and strong. This bond must come with an understanding of these mysteries which testifies that the one claiming foundation possesses the necessary understanding, knowledge and competency to work Quimbanda with agility and power.

Fundamento is also tied to lineage, some form of succession, and in truth the vinculum that needs to be in place is the triad between Exu, Tata and novice where the *fundamento* or power planted is set ablaze and can burn on its own. This is demonstrated through another saying in Brazil, that the one who has *fundamento* is the one who "throws a bottle of cachaça on the ground and from this 'the devil' is summoned". In other words it is about 'having Exu', that the bond between Tata and Exu is so strong that the powers are exercised with ease and precision. This in turn would indicate that solely possessing knowledge or a Spirit House is not enough, as the person claiming *fundamento* must also be truly hooked up into this force field.

This means that this connection can be established through years of working with Exu, a gradual process that layer by layer forges these bonds to be stronger and stronger. It can also be

---

7 *Farofa* is a triturate made from corn, cassava, manioc and other vegetables used as a base to make *padê*, food for Exu and Pomba Gira.

established directly, like a lightning bolt, which happens during a ritual induction, or what we might call initiation, to Quimbanda.

When we speak of initiation in relation to Quimbanda we must keep in mind that we are dealing with a living cult, hence the protocol for induction must be somewhat fluid and flexible as long as we follow the bones of the path, so to speak, and ensure that the secret steps that constitute the acts and deeds that generate foundation are performed. The bones of the path are the elements necessary to effectively bind the pact that is made, because in truth the 'initiation' takes the shape of a pact, and by pact we mean a contract written in earth, blood and fire that establishes a lifelong bond between entity and man.

Fundamento also becomes important in relation to where the Quimbanda in question is coming from. As we saw in the previous chapter and will explore further in the next, Quimbanda is simply a name for a denomination or cult where we find Exu and Pomba Gira at the centre, hence from this criterion we must accept the existence of a plurality of denominations. No matter the denomination, the ever-turning point is that you must 'have Exu', the connection with the spirit must be true and vibrant, hence no matter how a person comes to 'have Exu' the proof of possessing foundation is found in this bond.

After two decades of study and personal involvement with Quimbanda I have had the good fortune of becoming acquainted with many varieties of the cult, leading to my *fundamento* over the years becoming a patchwork of *fundamentos*, plural, with inductions, teachings and training from Quimbanda that came through Candomblé, through Umbanda and through the older houses of macumba, and even through an ancestral line, one Yaya being a fourth generation Quimbandeira originally from a Calundu, which was the term for a domestic cult of 'black magic' prefiguring Quimbanda in the early 1800s, in Cachoeira, Bahia.

What is interesting is that in all these instances the basic elements were the same; hence it was variations over the same *fundamento*. The presence of some form of physical vessel and the merging with Exu or Pomba Gira as a tutelary spirit or daimonic intelligence through various levels of possession do mark foundation.

Lastly, we need to address the matter of innovation, fabrication and visions of change, as it is in this realm, the more theological one, where I believe the bond between man and entity can be weak or strong, and hence we might say that a foundation can be weak or strong as well depending on one's truthfulness. This is a fine line to walk because since Quimbanda is a living cult it will change and shed its skin now and then, but as the snake doing the same will always be a snake, so it is also with Quimbanda, hence the change will be within given parameters that maintain the characteristics of Quimbanda which persist. Let us take two examples that seem to have been popular trends in recent years. One is to see Exu as a guardian spirit that operates under the command of Orixá to protect and serve humankind in the form of some astral police force. It is difficult to take a stand regarding this on the basis of right and wrong, save that the teachings I received about it were always the same. Exu is first and foremost the soul of dead people that continue to influence humans due to a resonance and sympathy whereby they can take on the role of a *guia* or guide. It was also thought that the 'proto-Exus', if you will, were aggressive cosmic forces that gave power to places, not unlike a genius loci forged in fire. When these principles are expanded upon into a conception of the Exus being an 'astral police force', something very strange happens, as the third point in the teachings I received was that Exu is amoral, that he never judges, that he is a devil that lives in the laughter of the nightclub and the darker parts of the world and society, hence if he is to be seen as a cop, it is an anarchic cop in revolt against temporal law and our moralistic ideas of crime and punishment. In the same vein we have the matter of Satanism, and Quimbanda is absolutely Satanic; after all, the plethora of spirits have fangs, horns, tails, cloven hoofs and are red of hue in their exhibitionistic display of flesh and pleasure. We are in this regard speaking of two forms of Satanism. Firstly it is the Satanism the Jesuits saw in their heretic converts in seventeenth-century Congo, and secondly a *fin de siècle*

Satanism as expressed, for instance, in Stanislaw Przybyszewski's *The Synagogue of Satan* published in 1897.

To cut to the chase, when the Jesuit mission tried to convert the Kongolese they were confronted with such massive theological problems that they eventually largely gave up on correcting the converts' heretical interpretations. These 'theological errors' were to a great extent related to the perception of power through the word *nkisi*. *Nkisi* simply means 'something of power' and can refer to a person or an object. Hence Jesus Christ was a *nkisi*, a talisman was a *nkisi*, a Christian saint was a *nkisi*, the king of the village was a *nkisi* and naturally Satan was also a *nkisi*. Not only this, but this *nkisi* of night, with horns and a tail, quite similar to some of the more protective and hostile wood spirits in the Kongo basin, would for people suffering at the hands of its colonizers be a proper and powerful *nkisi* to cultivate as a protection against those colonizers. This would happen within our without the Christian theological context, but more often Satan as *nkisi* was taken at face value, its own power, not so much antagonist to the solar *nkisi* Jesus Christ, as a *nkisi* that inspired fear amongst the enemy—hence, the enemy of my enemy might be my friend. We can see the memory of this in the iconography and in the *pontos cantados* of Exu and Pomba Gira even today, like in the following three famous *pontos cantados*:

> Exu que tem duas cabeças
> *Exu have two heads*
> Exu segura a banda com fé
> *Exu keeps faithfully his squad safe*
> Uma é Satanás do Inferno
> *One (head) is Satan from Hell*
> E a outra é de Jesus de Nazaré
> *The other is Jesus from Nazareth*
>
> Satanás, Satanás,
> *Satan, Satan,*

mataram o ferrabrás[8]
murdered the violent one
e quem confia no Diabo
who puts his trust in the Devil
a cada dia cresce mais
will grow more and more each day
e ai de mim se não fosse o Diabo
if it wasn't for me, it wasn't for the Devil
ai de mim se não fosse o Diabo
if it wasn't for me, it wasn't for the Devil
Saravá Exu tranca ruas
Salutations Exu Roadblocker
com sua marafa
with your booze
seu chifre e seu rabo
your horns and your tail

Plantei jiló
Planting eggplant
Nasceu quiabo
Up grew the Okra
Plantei jiló
Planting eggplant
Nasceu quiabo
Up grew the Okra
Que família é essa?
What Family is this?
É a família do Diabo
t is the Family of the Devil
Como é linda a família do Diabo
How the Family of the Devil is beautiful
Como e linda a família do Diabo
How the Family of the Devil is beautiful

---

8 Ferrabras is also a Saracen knight in medieval French tales, reputed for his courage and crude violence.

What we see in these *pontos* is the association with both Satan and the Devil on the premise that Exu is a *nkisi* forged in certain qualities. We see from the first *ponto* that there is no friction with, for instance, Christianity when it comes to Exu; on the contrary it appears that there is a full acceptance of how Satan is a necessary part of the Christian mythology. If we go to the second *ponto* we find several clues to the foundation of Quimbanda, that it is about trust with your Exu, that Exu have the power of taking down even seemingly overpowering opposition, and that Exu is 'the Devil'. The diabolism is taken to even more humorous lengths in the third *ponto* that speaks about how the path of Quimbanda is mysterious and beautiful, with the focus on the family ties important for gaining the trust of Exu, ties that frequently are defined as 'the pact'. It is quite evident that the diabolic imagery of Exu in the first place owes its form to the Kongolese idea of Satan in the guise in which he was presented by the Capuchins, and hence the image of this protective *nkisi*, horns and tail bathing in hellfire. This iconography was also an imagery proper for the aesthetics of the *fin de siècle* Satanism that took the Devil to the basement of the church, presiding over black masses and forbidden knowledge. But from the basement of the church in J.-K. Huysmans's Satanic masterpiece *Las Bas,* the Devil also went out in the streets of Rio de Janeiro as a hustler, a trickster, as a patron of the people of the street. It follows that decadence and dandyism influenced the perception of Exu, but the form of dandyism rooted in Baudelaire of which Albert Camus wrote in his 1951 publication *L'Homme révolté* the following:

> The dandy is, by occupation, always in opposition. He can only exist by defiance... The dandy, therefore, is always compelled to astonish. Singularity is his vocation, excess his way to perfection. Perpetually incomplete, always on the fringe of things, he compels others to create him, while denying their values. He plays at life because he is unable to live it.

We see from Camus an idea well-fitting to Exu and Pomba Gira as they express themselves in the nightside of life and pleasure, a form, as said, originally inspired by Baudelaire and in particular his 1857 poem *Litanies of Satan* which deserves to be quoted in full:

> *O you, the most knowing, and loveliest of Angels,*
> *a god fate betrayed, deprived of praises,*
> *O Satan, take pity on my long misery!*
> *O, Prince of exile to whom wrong has been done,*
> *who, vanquished, always recovers more strongly,*
> *O Satan, take pity on my long misery!*
> *You who know everything, king of the underworld,*
> *the familiar healer of human distress,*
> *O Satan, take pity on my long misery!*
> *You who teach even lepers, accursed pariahs,*
> *through love itself the taste for Paradise,*
> *O Satan, take pity on my long misery!*
> *O you who on Death, your ancient true lover,*
> *engendered Hope – that lunatic charmer!*
> *O Satan, take pity on my long misery!*
> *You who grant the condemned that calm, proud look*
> *that damns a whole people crowding the scaffold,*
> *O Satan, take pity on my long misery!*
> *You who know in what corners of envious countries*
> *a jealous God hid those stones that are precious,*
> *O Satan, take pity on my long misery!*
> *You whose clear eye knows the deep caches*
> *where, buried, the race of metals slumbers,*
> *O Satan, take pity on my long misery!*
> *You whose huge hands hide the precipice,*
> *from the sleepwalker on the sky-scraper's cliff,*
> *O Satan, take pity on my long misery!*
> *You who make magically supple the bones*
> *of the drunkard, out late, who's trampled by horses,*
> *O Satan, take pity on my long misery!*

> *You who taught us to mix saltpetre with sulphur*
> *to console the frail human being who suffers,*
> *O Satan, take pity on my long misery!*
> *You who set your mark, o subtle accomplice,*
> *on the forehead of Croesus, the vile and pitiless,*
> *O Satan, take pity on my long misery!*
> *You who set in the hearts and eyes of young girls*
> *the cult of the wound, adoration of rags,*
> *O Satan, take pity on my long misery!*
> *The exile's staff, the light of invention,*
> *confessor to those to be hanged, to conspirators,*
> *O Satan, take pity on my long misery!*
> *Father, adopting those whom God the Father*
> *drove in dark anger from the earthly paradise,*
> *O Satan, take pity on my long misery!*

It is quite astonishing to see how the perception of Satan as a healer of human distress and consoler of human misery is what stands out for Baudelaire, not different from how Satan must have appeared for the Kongolese, a powerful spirit that brought power, protection and comfort to those persecuted and accursed in the name of Jesus the *nkisi*. This common idea, however, found its own unique expression in Brazil where Exu continued to exist—in defiance and on the fringe of things—always as consoler of human misery.

As we see, the idea of foundation, to have Exu, ties into many factors, comprising a vinculum or bond with Exu, physical objects, and a precise knowledge and understanding. This leads to the final point to be made in this chapter, namely about innovation and tradition, and in this it is important to keep in mind that to make something your own is a quite different process from creating your own system. Tradition is continued by observing the protocol of cult and ensures that the essence of the cult remains intact. Quimbanda is diabolic and it continues West African ideas of power in the guise of a Devil forged from both European ideas and the Satan of the Church. Exu is earth and fire, the horns symbolize dominion, the exposed genitals and breasts freedom, the cloven hoof and human foot speaks of a being that stands with one foot in our world and the other in Hell, or the other side, this parallel reality that separate our worlds in two barely distinguishable frequencies. Every *cabula*, temple, house or *terreiro* of Exu will always make Quimbanda their own, to give it a distinct flavour and punch. Of course, some will also try to invent things and end up with a fragmented or broken bond with their Exu, because at the end of the night you either have *fundamento* or you don't. Each and every one in the solitude of the night knows who he or she is, and because of that Exu does not need anyone to defend him against anything; rather we must accept that in the world of Exu, the hustler, the charlatan, the trickster and the fool walk side by side with men and women of upright fire.

CHAPTER FOUR
On Hierarchies

As portas do inferno estremeceu
The gates of Hell were shaking
Todos correram para ver quem é
Everyone ran to see who it was
Eu dei uma gargalhada na encruzilhada
I gave a scream of laughter in the Crossroad
É a pomba gira e o compadre Lúcifer
It was Pomba Gira with her accomplice Lucifer
Eu dei a gargalhada na encruzilhada
I gave a scream of laughter in the Crossroad
É a pomba gira e o compadre Lúcifer
It was Pomba Gira with her accomplice Lucifer

The spirit hierarchies we find in Quimbanda are often modelled on feudal or military structures where we have a royal point at the top; in the case of Quimbanda this is the Maioral. The Maioral can be understood in metaphorical terms to be three shades of light as it moves in darkness; this gives way to the Maioral being understood through his immediate triune, the King Exus, which are Exu Lucifer, Exu Belzebub (also known as Exu Mor) and Astaroth (also known as Pomba Gira Figueira do Inferno, or just Pomba Gira do Inferno). After this some temples and liens operate with an Exu Rei, which will then be a synthesis of these powers in a lower, more tangible frequency. From this triune is actually created a diamond shape, if you see: the Maioral on top radiating into three zones of power is then absorbed again by Exu Rei that is both its own mystery and also an active force commanding other Exus. We might call this the infernal hierarchy or mystery of Quimbanda, where all sorts of Exus and Pomba Giras find their rank and role depending on what line we are speaking about and in what kingdom we happen to be. Let us take an example.

The Line of the Cemetery is ruled by Exu Caveira, Exu Skull, who then oversees this realm. His right and left hand are Exu Tata Caveira and Exu Brasa, Exu Burning Coal. But in the cemetery, we also have the Cruzeiro, which is the large central cross dedicated to ancestors, ruled by Exu do Cruzeiro. Also, in this line or realm we find Exu do Lodo who surfaces when the cemetery dirt gets wet and muddy and brings bones and coffin nails to the surface. Then we have Exu das Sombras, Exu of the Shadows, and Exu Asa Negra, Exu Black Wing, that make part of the line called Mossoroubi, hence it is in this chain of command under Kaminaloá they find rank, but they are also found in the cemetery as the particular places of power for Exu Asa Negra are the mounds or higher places in a cemetery, and Exu das Sombras is particularly powerful in the places at the cemetery where trees and tombs cast their shadow. If we add to this that at the gate of the cemetery we find Ogum Megé protecting this realm, we have an idea of how the hierarchies in Quimbanda work. Indeed, there is a hierarchy, but at the same time every single Exu and Pomba Gira has particular places in the world, what we call crossroads, where they are extremely powerful due to being the power of that place or phenomenon or energetic constitution. In addition we have the most important hierarchy, the one of the *cabula*, temple or *tronco* itself, because the Tata or Yaya who owns the *tronco*, i.e., temple, will naturally be subject to a unique and personal hierarchy of spirits related to how the Exu and Pomba Gira of the Tata or Yaya become the King and Queen of this particular *tronco*, and then the rest of the spirits follow in level and degree in conformity with which spirits want to work with the Tata or Yaya. This hierarchy may change due to the increase of people in the house, as every Quimbandeiro that joins a house will bring his or her spirits to the table; the hierarchies may or may not change, but the number of spirits will multiply. Basically, this means that in the temple of a Tata the hierarchy of the Exus is more like what we find in the *cosa nostra*, with the Exu or Pomba Gira of the Tata or

Yaya as the godfather of the squad or crew of spirits making up the retinue. From this the King and Queen of the temple have their Exus and Pomba Giras of trust and proximity who in turn have their Exus and Pomba Giras of resonance and preference. Hence, again, searching for the one true hierarchy besides the Maioral/Rei mystery will be as many things in Quimbanda when we set out to find the truth embedded in something rigid or dogmatic—a fool's errand. Let us present the most classic of all chains of command here, where I have made one substitution, placing Pomba Gira do Inferno as the third in command instead of Rei das Sete Encruzilhadas, King of the Seven Crossroads.

The Maioral
↓
Exu Lúcifer – First in command
↙ ↘
Put Satanakia – Exu Marabô   Agalieraps – Mangueira

Belzebub, Exu Mor – Second in command
↙ ↘
Tarchimache – Exu Tranca Ruas   Sagathana – Exu Veludo

Astaroth, Pomba Gira do Inferno – Third in command
↙ ↘
Fleurty – Exu Tiriri   Nesbiros – Exu dos Rios

Syrach – Exu Calunga – Gnomo – Kalunginha

I decided here to also leave the syncretism developed between some Exus and the demons in *Grimorium Verum*, simply due to Lucifer, Belzebub, and Astaroth being the three forces springing forth from the Maioral, whence it does make some sense to maintain the demonic references, at least in this first hierarchy. What I want to stress is that this hierarchy, if we strip away the religious connotation, is simply a chain of command equally valid for the spirit hierarchies of the Church as for the Roman organization of the military as it was used to organize the spirits in the grimoires. It is simply a taxonomy useful as a reference so we can understand more or less what the power balance is in the realm of Exu. But we need to take this imagery further, because even if Exu Tranca Ruas is the right arm of Exu Mor he is also a powerful general with legions of spirits under his command, and this is a truth for every single Exu and Pomba Gira. They are all legion, and thus we cannot understand these hierarchies apart from how they speak of a relationship of power between the Exus and Pomba Giras, but this does not reflect rank in terms of subordination and domination, as in the military. What we find at the crown of these legions, however, is the mysterious force referred to as 'the Maioral', the big guy, the guy in charge. This mystery is never manifested, as it is the cosmic source of all things Quimbanda. The Maioral is known through his three emissaries, Exu Lúcifer, Exu Belzebub and Pomba Gira do Inferno, whilst the *ponto* of the Maioral is a fusion of St. Michael the Archangel and the Orixá Ogum.

The most famous seal of the Maioral we have is the one published by Aluizio Fontenelle in his book *Exu* from 1951 and replicated on the following page. The idea behind the *ponto* of the Maioral is quite simple. For him, the seven legions or lines or the mystery of Quimbanda encoded in the number 7 is placed over the symbol of a waxing or waning Moon, referring to the night time. A triangle of manifestation is used as a backdrop for the swords of Ogun, but crowned by the Sun turns into a glyph of St. Michael syncretized with Ogun, the Orixá of iron, fire and blacksmithery. Also, in Yourba philosophy (Ifá) we should take note of how Ogun is understood to be the force that controls the *ajoguns* (spirits of misfortune), he himself being the creator of the human spine and the one that made paths on earth and between earth and heaven. Now, I don't know if Fontenelle knew about this factor, but what is known is that he somehow saw a relationship between Ogun and St. Michael and thus encoded this mystery in the *ponto* of Exu Rei as a reference to the mystery of the Maioral. Knowing that in the early days of Umbanda adopting Quimbanda, Ogun was seen as the regulator and protector of Quimbanda, the pieces start to fall into place.

This means that saying Ogun is the Maioral is not correct, nor is it correct to say St. Michael is; rather it is that nameless mystery that makes one reflect the other of which the Maioral speaks—and if we understand St. Michael as he is and strip down the Christian bias, we find that the Bogomils of the Balkans believed that Michael was actually the creation of Satanael, yet sanctioned by God. Also, we need to stress that the Bogomils were persecuted because of their doctrine concerning the godhood. For them there was one God above, immaterial and aloof, the golden Tzar, and one god on earth, that actually could make use of matter, the Silver Tzar, Satanael. Hence, when we look at heresies like this and see that Michael is a spirit of fire that is primarily concerned with exorcisms, it does speak clearly about how intimate he is with the 'demonic' realm and how his understanding of this darker spirit world is so great that he literally keeps the demons under his cape, as the godson of Satanael he truly is… If we add to this that to exorcise is really not about casting out spirits per se, but impurities at large that attach themselves to everything, our idea of St. Michael as a proper icon for the Maioral does make sense.

Another hierarchy we often find in Quimbanda, clearly an Umbanda legacy yet the principles behind it tend to make sense when we are speaking of these spirits we call Exu and Pomba Gira, is the transition from pagan to baptised to crowned. This is usually interpreted as bringing the spirit from darkness to light, but in truth we are speaking of a maturity of spirit. This is because there is a tendency of finding it problematic to control one's Exu at first; we ask things, nothing happens, we feel we sometimes have connection and other times just silence, and sometimes a work even prematurely gives results, but far from what we wanted to achieve. All these factors speak of a 'pagan' or immature relationship, and it is only in working a spirit, using the format of communion, training mediumship, and understanding the balance between talking and giving, that the spirit becomes 'baptised'—and this also reflects itself in a greater maturity of the practitioner as well. A 'crowned' condition means that the Exu manifests in stable and good ways and takes on the role of a Tata or teacher of the Quimbandeiro. It has little to do with bringing a spirit from darkness to light; rather it is about maturation of a relationship.

All this aside, the true hierarchy of Quimbanda is the hierarchy that is established at your *tronco* using your personal spirit court as reference. This means for the individual practitioner his or her personal Exu and Pomba Gira will gradually take the role of King and Queen of the *tronco*. As they grow in power one of the three generals (masked under Belzebub, Lucifer and Astaroth or the corresponding Exus) tends to establish themself in mysterious ways as a focal point of the King and Queen, gradually taking on the virtues of the Maioral under this particular form and guise. This is for sure a mystery that will mature in time although I believe the mystery of the Maioral is intentionally something that should remain somehow veiled, because mystery, fire and earth is the very nerve of Quimbanda.

The dynamic beneath how the hierarchy of the *tronco* establishes itself also explains why every 'casa de Exu' is different from any other. The expression of the house is born from the court of spirits establishing itself at the *tronco*, and in this the teachings of the spirits. This means that when Exu teaches people of a particular *cabula* or house, this is for that house and is never a generic teaching for Quimbanda at large; these teaching are limited to the particular house. What ties all houses together are the commonalities of how an *assentamento* is made, how the pact with a spirit is made and the importance placed upon the relationship with Tata Exu. Even in this there are great variations, yet there will always be an inherent kernel of similarity that ties Quimbanda to Quimbanda across the diversity of the many houses, temples, *tendas* and *cabulas*. Hence, we see from this that any discourse speaking of right or wrong Quimbanda is futile and would more reveal a weak understanding of this art or a less than honest connection with deceptive spirits that seek to control. We are here touching a bit upon the field of spirit imposters, *kiumbas* and larvae, but we will leave that for later and rather emphasize that the hierarchy of Quimbanda is unique to the house, as every *tronco* is unique and every practitioner different, so this difference is expressed from house to house, yet we find commonalities that enable us to recognize the great variety of Quimbanda for what it is.

CHAPTER FIVE

The Syntax of Quimbanda

A porta do inferno estremeceu
Gate to Hell was shaking
Veio todo mundo para ver quem é
veryone came to see who would arrive
Era João Caveira
It was John Skull
Com a mulher de Lúcifer
With the Woman of Lucifer

Quimbanda is at its core a reflex of the sorcerous spirituality we find amongst Kimbundu-speaking people in Angola and Bantu-speaking people in the vast lands we call Kongo. But nothing is ever that simple in Brazil. Again, we need to revisit the idea of power and sorcery at large.

If we look at the research done by Edison Carneiro (1912–1972), and later Roger Bastide (1898–1974), some level of irritation is expressed by both regarding macumba. Whilst for Carneiro the irritation is more related to the difficulties of finding the multiple roots and influences of macumba, Bastide, following in the research of Carneiro, quite simply in the name of 'low spiritism' dismissed macumba and its syncretism as something marginal and degenerated, lowly and sorcerous, as all Bantu cults were for him. Bastide was himself made to the Orixá Xangô in the traditional Candomblé Nagô *terreiro Axe Opo Afonjá* in Salvador, Bahia, which he himself found to be the most authentic and 'pure' African legacy. Since Bastide was on the search for authenticity and African legacies, he had a tendency to look down on what he saw as primitive and 'low' magic. Yet it is here, in the 'low spiritism' and the rich syncretism of Bantu cults, that macumba evolved, and it is here we find the syntax of Quimbanda. As professor of anthropology Waldemar Valente wrote:

> The phenomenon of syncretism appeared early on due to the conflict-ridden situations imposed on people due to the shock of conglomeration between the African fetishism and the Iberic-Brazilian Catholicism. On one side, it was contrasting religions, diverse and true in themselves, but they also crossed over due to several points of communality and identification, especially through the traces of common fetishism.[9]

This 'common fetishism' refers to something that has already been commented on, namely the concept of *nkisi*, something of power in addition to the similarities that made people of the most varied spiritual backgrounds make connections and bond over different takes on shared mysteries. The most obvious syncretism we find between folk Catholicism and African faiths would be the syncretism between saints and Orixás, a syncretism that is not as uniform as one would like it to be. Let us take Xangô as an example. This Orixá is a famous Yorubá king and the chief deity of Oyo state in Nigeria. The cultic practices from this region crossed over to Brazil in the early 1800s to such an extent that in Pernambuco the votaries of what came to be known as Candomblé a few decades into the 1800s were known as *xangozeiros*. In Nigeria this Orixá was associated with kingship, the double-headed axe, fire, and with thunderstones. In Brazil his association with stones in general became embossed on his form more than any other feature. In Brazil he became known as the 'thrower of stones', 'the divine meteor', 'shower of boulders'. Hence, he became known by the colour brown and not the traditional blood-red colour he is known by in Yorubaland. Following the transformation of Xangô, we find him syncretised with St. Jerome due to this saint being famous for struggling with his temper and punishing himself

---

9 *Sincretismo Religioso Afro-Brasileiro*, Companhia Editora Nacional, 1977: p. 13 (trans. by Nicholaj de Mattos Frisvold).

for his errors by beating his chest with stones. The presence of stones we also find in the syncretism with Moses and his tablets of stone inscribed by divine fire, which would emphasize fire and stones as Xangô's most salient attributes. If we add to this ideas like Xangô the Younger and Xangô the Elder we also find that St. John's midsummer fire is sacred to Xangô the Younger, hence emphasizing the fiery disposition in the younger Xangô, in parallel to the association with stones and boulders in the Elder Xangô. Moreover, Xangô is the chief of seven legions of *caboclos*, the spirits of Native people, and each of these *caboclos* are working with a particular Exu. The line of Xangô is like this:

1st Legion – Caboclo Xangô Kaô – Exu Gira Mundo
(Caboclo salutations Xangô) (Exu Worldturner)

2nd Legion – Caboclo Xangô Pedra Branca – Exu Mangueira
(Caboclo Xangô White Stone) (Exu of the Mango Tree)

3rd Legion – Caboclo Xangô Agodô – Exu Pedreira
(Caboclo Xangó of 'secret fires') (Exu of the Quarry)

4th Legion – Caboclo Xangô Sete Montanhas – Exu Corcunda
(Caboclo of the Seven Mountains) (Exu Hunchback)

5th Legion – Caboclo Xangô Sete Cachoeiras – Exu Calunga
(Caboclo of the Seven Riverfalls) (Exu Calunga)

6th Legion – Caboclo Xangô Pedra Preta – Exu Meia-Noite
(Caboclo of the Black Stone) (Exu Midnight)

7th Legion – Caboclo Xangô Sete Pedreiras – Exu Ventania
(Caboclo of the Seven Quarries) (Exu of Strong Winds)

At this point there are several interpretations concerning how to understand these power relations. Personally, I do favour the idea that the Exus in this context are in a natural harmony with these *caboclos*, hence they represent the diurnal and nocturnal sides of the powers of the legion in question. Other ideas widespread are that the Exus are serving the *caboclos*, either because they are in need of spiritual evolution or just because they are inferior, perhaps a continuation of the view held by Bastide and others concerning the 'degenerated' Bantu cults. Naturally, from a Quimbanda perspective Exu and Pomba Gira are not spirits we seek to indoctrinate or elevate spiritually since we are embracing these forces as tutelary spirits and guides. In this way the elevation taking place is the simultaneous evolution or growth of medium and guide.

It is important to be aware of all these modalities for understanding Quimbanda and how legions of amoral spirits and entities can be interpreted in a great variety of different forms, all of them being correct in their own way, albeit some being healthier and more useful for one's life than others. Given the amoral nerve, it is also natural that we get what we expect with these entities, and in this the type of relationship we build will also impact our life and the spirit bond in exact, personal and peculiar ways. In my vision of Quimbanda we are dealing with amoral fire taking root in the earth, and so it follows that Quimbanda is very much about mastering fire in all the possible nuances of both fire and mastery, with being consumed by fire or dominating it being the two natural polarities of achievement. By being consumed by fire I mean being consumed by anger, vengeance and other hot emotions that are often a reaction upon injustice witnessed or suffered, which is just all too human. A very important point to keep in mind regarding this is that most Exus and all Pomba Giras transmigrated into these forms of entities due to personal histories involving anger, vengeance and other forms of fiery emotions. This means that in their capacity as teachers they will always be interested in showing 'the other way', as they themselves, when they disincarnated, did so because they went with the fiery impulses and suffered death as a consequence. Their amoral nature causes them to never push anything upon anyone, lest asked, and when asked and their opinion is given, the responsibility is upon the one who asked to follow up or not. The exception here is the factor of trade, pact and the contract. If something is promised for a work done, this must be given without delay or reservation as this is the second salient feature with Exu and Pomba Gira after the amoral disposition. This means that 'the law' of Quimbanda is one that goes beyond Good and Evil, and naturally it takes a certain level of self-awareness—if not cosmic awareness—to bond with spirits like this in a benign way, which is why so many prefer to work with Exu in relation to *pretos-velhos*, Orixás, or *caboclos*: it brings in a safety net and some level of protection, which for many might be a very wise step to take.

The Exus themselves also form their own hierarchies, defining how they stand with one another but also where in the world they have their power and influence. We must understand that the Exus are a conglomerate of two spiritual ideas, the crossroad and the dead. The crossroad typifies any junction where transition is made and power is found, hence the crossroad is the place where the entity comes into his or her power. For instance, Exu of the Mango Tree would naturally be found at this tree, but also giving this Exu offerings of this tree, either carved tools or its fruits, would enhance the presence of this Exu. Not only this, but the mango tree is also the tree where the mythical forest being *Curupira* prefers to stay. Curupira is a guardian spirit of the forest, cunning in sorcery and mischief, known by his backward-turned feet, loud shrieks in the night, and hair made from fire. Let us have a look at the *ponto* of Exu Mangueira in this regard:

> Ventou bem forte
> *The wind blew strong*
> A Mangueira nem tremeu
> *The mango tree not even shook*
> Quando ouviu sua gargalhada
> *When his laugher was heard*
> Todo mundo estremeceu
> *Everyone was shaken*
> Cuidado gente, Exu Mangueira

Careful people, Exu of the Mango Tree
É Quimbandeiro
is a Quimbandeiro
Santo Antônio dê Licença
St. Anthoy gave permission
Pra ele entrar neste terreiro
For him to come to this temple
Exu criado no meio da Bruxaria
Exu born in the midst of witchcraft
É um Exu enquizilado
Is an Exu much sought after
É melhor tomar cuidado
Better be careful
Sabe tudo de magia
He knows all about magic

This *ponto* is quite interesting, as the motifs of Curupira, that the wind can't touch him and that he knows all forms of sorcery, are used to describe this mighty and powerful forest Exu that is given access to the *terreiro* or temple due to the intervention of St. Anthony who is inviting him. St. Anthony is syncretised with Ogum, but is quite often viewed to be, beneath the monk's frock, an Exu himself, more precisely Exu Pemba, the Exu of chalk and signatures. It is quite amazing to see how we find Exu and Pomba Gira everywhere and how they manage to stand in good relationships with saints, *caboclos*, Orixás and *pretos-velhos*, not as a hostile element, but as a force of transformation that get things done, and this often with a sense of humour and some deep life wisdom, while generating a sense of danger fused with feeling good and accepted.

It is exactly this amoral transformative essence that enables Exu to find his place everywhere with agility and in acceptance. Exu, the friend of saints, fallen angels, *caboclos, pretos-velhos* and Orixás is also the friend of those he comes down to meet, greet and work with in the *terreiro*. It is in Exu's ability to synthesize and form alliances that we find the true power of Quimbanda.

This power comes from the primordial ideas of the hunter societies, and we should also keep in mind that this word, Kongo or Nkongo, in Bantu does mean 'hunter'. But in traditional societies the hunter was not someone shooting game for sport; there was so much more to it than this. The hunter was in charge of rites of passage, of surgery, of forging tools and weapons, and was also a medicine man, sorcerer and healer because this was indispensable knowledge to possess in order to track down game and maintain health and vigour out in the savannah and jungle across days or weeks. This hunter origin will also explain why the importance of Ogum used to be so strong in Quimbanda. It was Ogum that gave permission to the Exus to use his powers for whatever end. Even if today Ogum has fused his function as 'Tyler at the Door' with suchlike as Exu Porteira or Exu Tranca Ruas, the mark Ogum placed on Quimbanda is undeniable. The red-hot peppers, the tobacco, the iron, the fire, the strong drinks are all important elements in the cult of Ogum in West Africa. We can, however, wonder why this Kongo-derived cult decided to implement a Yoruba Orixá, since this power existed in Angola and Kongo under the name of Nkosi or Incoce, a word meaning 'lion'. The domain of Nkosi is the same as that of Ogum, but one aspect is enhanced greatly, Nkosi's ability to open roads and cross over from one path to another. These paths and roads he was opening served as gateways for the spirits called Pombajira, a word that in Bantu and Kimbundu (pambu ia-njila) means 'crossroads'. Pombajira, this serpentine and wet spirit, became in time known as Pomba Gira, whilst Exu was the name given to the other form of crossroad spirit called Aluvaia, considered the guardian of communication, language and social order.

The memory of the hunter societies we also find in the early manifestations of *'mbanda'* as spoken of by Archbishop Nery in the state of Espirito Santo in the late seventeenth century. The *macumbeiros* of *mbanda* went out in the forest with a single candle to attract their Tata/spirit, and depending on the qualities of the Tata the hunter shaman came back with he was recognized as either a healer or a poisoner in the *ngira* or celebration. We find in this account also a hint about going out in the woods to find what is yours, the spirit that resonates with you, a concept that turned into the personal and working spirits in the court of Quimbanda—or, if we assess the material at our disposal, was already there as a guiding line for the *mbandeiros* and *macumbeiros*.

Quimbanda is at root about realizing power and its uses, and this is not only limited to minerals, animals or plants, but also to the idea and virtue that gives a given spirit a name and presence. Hence Quimbanda is about understanding all the crossroads of power we can find in the world, seen and invisible.

Chapter Six
Quimbanda Spirits

O sino da igrejinha faz
The bell of the little church made
Belém, blem, blom
Belém, blem, blom
Deu meia-noite, o galo já cantou
At mid-night the rooster was crowing
Seu Tranca Ruas que é o dono da gira
Mr. Tranca Ruas is the owner of the gira
Oi corre gira que Ogum mandou
oh, let the gira flow, the gira Ogum authorized

It should by now be quite evident why there seems to be so much disagreement amongst Quimbandeiros about who is Exu, who is Pomba Gira and what is the one true Quimbanda. It is quite simply a natural reflex of these spirits that are tied to crossroads, power and communication, this volatile mercurial element that rolls around in the dampness of earth taking fire. Let us continue some of the threads in the previous chapters and tie them together here as we move on towards further clarifications and the more practical aspects of the cult.

The first ambiguity we should address is the fusion of Exu, Èṣú and Devil. The most popular perception these days is to firmly state that Èṣú is not Exu and that Exu is not the Devil, but I would say this is not that simple. Let us take some salient virtues that these three entities or deities have in common:

Exu	**Èṣú**	**The Devil**
Crossroads	Crossroads	Crossroads
Choices	Choices	Choices
Fire	Fire	Fire

Nocturnal	Nocturnal	Nocturnal
Pantomath	Pantomath	Pantomath
Trickster	Trickster	Trickster
Loyal	Loyal	Loyal
Mercury	Mercury	Mercury

If we look at the differences between Exu and the Orixá Èṣú understood from his context in Ifá, things shape up in interesting ways. In Ifá, Èsú is indeed a mercurial figure that holds the indispensable role of delivering prayers and sacrifice to Olodumare, the owner of the World. He is the confidant of Orunmila, the spirit of Wisdom, and his place is at the crossroads where he watches all events on earth unfolding. Èṣú is also in possession of a sacred club that he punishes people with, as he is also an instigator of confusion as a means for teaching people about good character. This ambiguity of Èṣú, combined with his necessity in making anything work, generated in many houses of Candomblé in Brazil the idea that Èṣú was a force that had to be appeased in order not to generate confusion in the ritual and magical works of the *terreiro*. Hence the idea of feeding Èṣú first comes from this attitude of keeping this force away, whilst in Ifá Èṣú is fed first because he is the one that understands both the human situation and the celestial situation and thus serves as a bridge (i.e. crossroad) between the visible and invisible realms. But it is in the elements of cult that we see a great departure from Èṣú to Exu. In Quimbanda we use several forms of hot peppers, most of which are taboo for Èṣú, and tobacco, another taboo for Èṣú. These elements however are, as commented earlier, intrinsic to the cultivation of the Orixá Ogun/Ogum. And if we pause here and reflect upon how Ogun has managed to take prominent roles in Afro-derived cults, always as the owner of sorcery, a hunter, a warrior, we can see in the imagery of Ogun the primordial icon of the hunter. Hence Exu borrows elements from both of these forces in order to become his very own 'man', owner of his own cult. This leaves us the Devil to clarify, besides the obvious syncretism taking place in the Capuchin mission in West Africa where Orixás like Èṣú and Ogun were by definition 'devils' and 'demons', especially Èṣú whose shape with horns and a massive phallus would of course remind the missionaries of the Devil who visited the witches at their Sabbath. But there is an entire other view to this that should be clear as we take a more objective stance on the matter. Firstly, the Devil, when he figures in the Bible to tempt people, does so under divine dictate. When he makes Job suffer, it was God who allowed it; when he tempted Jesus in the desert, it was God who allowed it; when he executes punishment, it is done due to God's judgment. Hence, the Devil is performing his function, a function which Sufi master Ibn Arabi defined as 'the limit of God's unfolding'. Another factor is that the Devil knew things... He knew about the great secrets of the world and creation, and he knew how to heal, how to curse, how to make the human life better and more interesting. After all, isn't he truly the King of the World, Light of the World?

And it is in this way Quimbanda becomes so beautiful, deep and bewildering, in its astute acceptance of the plethora of existence where the good and the bad are simply vectors we give to phenomena, born from our own moralism and personal judgment. Exu welcomes all, and hence we see how the Maioral happily takes the form of Belzebub and how his right hand Exu accepts the idea of Exu Lucifer with laughter and grace. This is because the diabolic form does challenge us, and as crossroad spirits, challenge is what they do. It is in this way we should understand the presence of 'demonic' entities from *Grimorium Verum* finding themselves in this realm as close cousins to the Exus. Quite proper to the history of Quimbanda, the syncretism with the demons from the *Verum* was most likely imposed by Aluizio Fontenelle who saw a way of dumping all things satanic into one place and making it all subject to the control of saints and Orixás, so what started as a prejudice became true and interesting.

In bringing these ideas together it would be illuminating to share what a medium incorporating a Pomba Gira related about them, as recorded in Liana Trindade's *Exu: Poder e Perigo*:

> I am eternal, because every Exu in the infernal current, is eternal. I am good, I help who deserves. If you give me what I want, I will help. It is not what I need, because I have the entire chthonic realm, the shadows for me. Because everything that exists on earth, the marihuana, the confusion, it is my kingdom…The horse (medium) doesn't like me, ok. Because he will never allow himself to do the things I do. Because if it was up to me, we would have toads, snakes, marihuana, everything to work. He doesn't want any of this, because his saint (Orixá) is not permitting him.
>
> When a woman gets lost (in desire) I laugh, when a man becomes effeminate, I also laugh because my world is so very beautiful. For me everything is good, because I have nothing to lose. I don't fight with the other Exus, because they have the Maioral to obey. We have Lucifer and we have Maria Padilha, they are king and queen. The other Exus are their slaves, the 'maioral' of the others, dominating them.[10]

From these words we see clearly the nature of Exu and Pomba Gira, how they are beyond good and evil and how they highlight the beauty of the world as it is, and the importance of using the world—toads, drugs, warts and all. Naturally this concept can generate some moral dilemmas on a human level, but this is also a part of the function of Exu.

And then lastly, Exu as we know him from the cult of Quimbanda has Bantu roots and was earlier known as Aluvaia and Pambujila, both names referring to a red force dwelling at the crossroad. If we look at Bantu cosmology, we find that Nzambi (god) indeed created crossroad spirits, spirits in charge of particular places of power in the world, and in particular the woods. This means that a primordial form of what we today call Exu was once upon a time a guardian of, for instance, the pine tree. This tree having a particular virtue was reflected in the essence of its

---

10 1985, p. 127 (trans. by Nicholaj de Mattos Frisvold).

guardian. As a tree grows and dies, turns into earth and is reborn in a different form, so it was with these crossroad spirits, they grow and increase through the death and decay encoded in nature.

Hence, we find here the only agreement amongst Quimbandeiros concerning the nature of Exu, that they are spirits linked to death, but in this particular context we've now spoken about, death as increase and root of legions. This also means that amongst the Exus we have spirits primordial and original that were at the same time the first created and the first dead, like Exu Sete Porteiras, Exu Sete Estrelas, Exu Mor and a few others.

Likewise, it follows that the first Exus we heard about in Brazil were all wood spirits, which is quite natural given the secret lore of how the Exus came to earth, and with wood spirits we speak of spirits wild, untamed, with fire on their heels. To bring your Tata out from the woods was to bring fire from darkness and allow yourself to get possessed by this particular spirit because in this union the Tata was able to transmit *força* and wisdom to its child.

And it is in this simple field things get complicated. Since Quimbanda is a cult focused on the secret of possession, we also need to understand the nuances and mechanisms of spirit possession, which will be the topic in our next chapter. For now we should just address the fact that merging with your Tata is based upon a harmony, hence the medium will always be a fusion of what it is, a composite of man and spirit, man and death, and the more we silence our own voice the more room we give to the 'other'.

But let us now follow the track of death as a format of expansion. Death causes us to unite with earth, and our virtues enter into harmony with pre-existing and existing virtues and intelligences, hence death and rebirth is about increase and expansion, and just as early man came out from their caves and gardens to build cities and spread across the earth in a variety of kingdoms, so did the Exus and Pomba Giras spread out into kingdoms. In the same manner it is with the dead ones. A person living a type of life typified by the qualities of a given Exu will upon death partly join with this *força*, this legion, and in time become an autonomous representative for a given virtue. This means that when person X calls Exu Veludo, for instance, he might act slightly different from how he appears to person Y; there will be a commonality addressing the 'Veludo-ness', but the type of spirit, the soul of death attached to it, can give a different reflection of what is basically the same spirit. This beautiful spiritual dynamic is what makes people quarrel about authenticity, and at the end it is only those who do not quarrel about this that have a genuine contact with their Tata, because when you know what you have, you have no need to impose yourself nor prove yourself...

And so there we are, crossroad upon crossroad, denoting the expansive and wise nature of these spirits. This is further emphasized by the true content of what we today call lines. In the past these lines denoted different varieties of making Quimbanda. You had Quimbanda that was from the woods, from the Mossorubi (Muslims), from the Nagô (Yoruba), that spoke of a particular modus operandi and approach to the mysteries. In the past the Exus and Pomba Giras involved in a particular line were the spirits you would be working with, as it made up your lineage of spirits and defined some form of protocol involved in this. Nowadays the Exus might speak of this and assign us a lineage denomination to uphold this memory, yet it all has become fused into a maze of kingdoms and lines that cross over everywhere. We can become nostalgic with such developments, or we can see in this the nature of Brazil and its people at work, which is about welcoming any melting pot as a good thing. Yet in doing this it is also good to know the root and route of how it came to be the way it is.

So, contemporary Quimbanda accepts that the Exus and Pomba Giras are spirits of the dead, many of them had lives before and they stay close to earth and humans both because of affinity and for tutorship—but also because at root they are guarding something of power. Hence, we find today the kingdoms of Quimbanda to be the realms of power open to us, be it the Cruzeiro, Calunga, Crossroads, the Ocean shore, Lyre or Woods; we see that places of power are places of movement, action or mystery, which means that any place or any death touched by these elements is potentially a place of power.

In this field we have the concept of kiumbas. Kiumba is a Kikongo word meaning 'skull', in the sense of this skull being empty and thus an empty vessel which can be filled with anything—like a lost soul not finding its way up or down—and remains confused and/or destructive. This quality of spirit—the lost soul or the hungry ghost—is what is known as a kiumba. These spirits are better chased away by salt, gunpowder and thyme thrown over your shoulder if you feel them try to attach themselves, or gather these elements in four vessels placed in the four corners of the house. Baths of thyme and sea salt also expel such intrusions. Such spirits can also be worked and even seated, but at this stage it is better to get rid of such energies.

Kiumbas are also known as *obsessores*, obsessive spirits or larvae, and some of them can have a fairly hot inclination towards being known or present, almost like the Jewish dybbuk. We know we are in touch with such energies when we feel an excess of negative emotions, be it jealousy, anger, sloth or the like, and when under such influence we also tend to be docile and indulge in self-sabotage. Naturally, such spirits can be put to use, but as said it is better to get rid of them in the way described. In addition, acts of charity tend to have a purifying effect when such energies seek to make themselves a part of our lives, so be generous and give to beggars with frequency if such instances occur.

As we see, Exu and Pomba Gira are primordial spirits ultimately rooted in their position as guardians of places of power, that have increased and spread due to the mysterious effect of death that embraces and renews its own power in its regeneration through multiple rebirths. Hence a true Exu or Pomba Gira will always be tied to this triad of wisdom, death and crossroads as something good and positive, yet hard to tackle because a guardian will always be a pyre of fire shooting up from the earth, and it is not always so easy to handle fire.

Some have seen a correlation between jinns and the Exus, and to some extent this is true, but while a jinn is made from smokeless fire, an Exu is the ambiguity of earth-fire, Fire resting in Saturn that speaks of another mystery. For the sake of analogy it might be useful to see the Exus as cousins of the jinns, yet we must keep in mind that jinns were created as a species apart; the Exus were created with a purpose to oversee, namely as guardians. As they guard their places of power they also guard their children as points of future power…

Chapter Seven
On Possessions

Ele vem, ele vem, ele vem
He arrives, he arrives, he arrives
Ele vem é de outro mundo
He arrives from the Other world
É Seu Tata Caveira
It is Mr. Tata Caveira
Ele vem quebrando tudo
He arrives breaking everything

Quimbanda is a cult rooted in the importance of possession; it is about spirit trafficking and allowing immaterial spirits to use our body and consciousness. Possession can for some be a fearful matter, given the idea of possession arriving to us from horror movies using hauntings and exorcisms as their backdrop.

Possessions as they take place in Quimbanda are phenomena as known both in Kardec's Spiritism, the *mesa branca*, as well as a traditional African modality of interacting with spirits.

The *mesa branca* when it came to Brazil was something reserved for aristocrats and people of some wealth. What else they had in common was their European heritage; black people or those of mixed blood were as unwelcome to most of these gatherings as their spirits were. The usual practice in the *mesa branca* if some non-Christian, non-Caucasian/European spirit tried to enter the table was to expel and exorcize the spirit. The *mesa branca* was truly a 'white table'.

The interesting aspect here is that the Kardecists were well aware of the possessions of African and native spirits (*caboclos*) and dismissed these spirits as inferior and the entire African modality as was performed in the houses of macumba as 'low spiritism'.

And it was in this field that Zélio de Morais contributed to a great change if not a greater survival of 'low spiritism', 'macumba', and what we today know as Quimbanda, by allowing 'low spiritism' to become the root of what he called Umbanda. Hence Zélio, being a white man and medium for the *preto-velho* Pai Antonio and the *caboclo* Sete Encruzilhadas, became an important bridge for the survival of macumba, and we might see Umbanda as important in this regard. Zélio's Umbanda was based upon charity and was free from racism and prejudice. His kind affinity with the African line is found in the name he chose, Umbanda, the act of healing, a Kimbundu word that in Angola is actually the practice of the Quimbanda (a traditional spiritual practitioner); hence the Quimbanda is doing Umbanda, the healer is doing healing.

So what we see here is that Spiritism and macumba were both cults or practices signified by possession, and the great difference was apparently in what type of spirits and what type of ancestors and dead ones were given passage; hence the distinction between 'high spiritism' and 'low spiritism' was in reality a racist separation, and 'low spiritism' was just another name for macumba, where *caboclos*, Exus and *pretos-velhos* were allowed to manifest. It is only natural that in this Franco-dominated spiritual legacy that came to Brazil, and in particular to Rio de Janeiro, at the time the capital of Brazil, the distinction between high/white and low/black magic as presented by Eliphas Levi melded with the ideas contained within high and low spiritism respectively.

So, what we find at the root of it all is prejudice and racism, but also these attempts at unification, partly made by the Freemasons, but in a way brought to fruition with the all-embracing attitude of Umbanda. Now, more than one hundred years after these definitions were first loaded with a racist content, this is not so anymore, but it is still important to be aware of the history of the words we are using and that how a nation defined things 100 years ago is not the way we define them today. An example of this is found also in the posture of the Roman Catholic Church in regard to Umbanda, what was known as 'the spiritism of Umbanda'. Spiritism was considered a heresy, and in Brazil it was in particular the monk Boaventura Kloppenburg that took upon himself the role of speaking against the heresy of Spiritism in general, and the 'low spiritism' of Umbanda in particular. In 1953 Kloppenburg instigated a Catholic campaign against the 'spiritism of Umbanda' due to its Catholic-Spiritist syncretism. After all, Jesus Christ was the owner of Umbanda, which rubbed Kloppenburg the wrong way, finding it as absurd to say you were Catholic and Spiritist as to say you were Catholic and Muslim at the same time. His agitations evaporated, however, towards the second Vatican council in 1962 where the Church toned down its attacks and diminished Spiritism in a Christian context to be more an error than a heresy. This shift was perhaps partly due to the neo-Pentecostal movement growing, since having a Christian faction receiving nothing less than the Holy Spirit itself made it difficult to uphold such a strict stance against receiving spirits with the blessing of Jesus Christ—not to mention that the Church itself has a long history of saints receiving 'holy inspiration' in various forms and degrees of intensity.

But, let us go to the topic, namely possession and how to develop mediumship. Both Spiritism and Umbanda have in this respect good strategies for developing mediumship, and to locate good centres to train this ability is a good thing, but for the sake of our topic, Quimbanda, we will adapt this storehouse of practice and knowledge to our purpose of giving passage to Exus and Pomba Giras. Now, it is important to stress the importance of ancestors in this, and so it is important to erect a shrine for ancestors and also one for Exu and Pomba Gira. A shrine serves as a place of comfort for spirits; just as we prepare a table for guests to arrive and feel comfortable and satisfied, so we do for our invisible friends by making their tables and shrines.

To erect an ancestor shrine is a quite simple matter. The *boveda* as exercised in Caribbean Spiritism can with good benefit be adapted for our purposes. Such a shrine is made by placing a small table in a corner of the house, and covering this with a white tablecloth. This can also be done directly on the floor if that is more suitable. On this table a glass of water is placed, which is flanked by one cup of sweet coffee and one glass of sweet liqueur. Preferences of departed family members when they were alive should be taken into account and the offerings mediated accordingly. For instance, if alcoholism was a trait of your grandfather, you might water down the alcohol or substitute the liquor with a glass of milk, adding a few spoons of red wine or whiskey. On the table you place symbols indicative of your ancestry, i.e. a nail for blacksmiths, monopoly money for bankers, a bible for priests and the clergy and so forth. You will have white candles present on the table and elect one day a week, preferably at the same hour, to do this. At first you will simply present the offerings and light the candles, knock three times on the table and say: '*Blood of my blood, Spirits of my Spirit. Ancestors known and unknown, it is me NN that is calling you. I am offering you to drink with me and to stay with me. In doing this I know you will stay closer to me, protect me and teach me.*'

In the beginning you will simply stay there for a designated time, like thirty minutes in meditation, being receptive. You can name your ancestors if you know their names; if not, rest assured your ancestors will recognize you. As the flow starts to happen, you will start composing poetry to your ancestors, celebrating their good deeds, be they imaginary—as in cases when one's ancestors are not known—yet still born from the inspiration happening at the table, or actual qualities of known individuals. Even difficult ancestors would have at least one quality worthy of praise, so try to avoid bitterness or resentment in this, give a quick praise for ancestors you are not feeling well about, and focus on those you have a stronger link with. This is a gradual process and visions, dreams, sensations and inspirations can all guide the way further.

It is not necessary to enter into possession with one's ancestors *per se* but it is always good to have this support with us when we work with disincarnated spirits.

Possession is a gradual process that starts with training our sensibility for vibrations. It is advisable to have an assistant when working with possession and to take turns in the process.

As for training our mediumship, let us start with the simple things and avoid complications. Some people are more naturally inclined towards mediumship than others, yet having the sensibility towards vibrations is always good, hence psychometrics are always helpful in order to train our awareness of what lies near at hand, veiled from our sight, but sensed by other faculties. In this way we develop our intuition, and gradually we will start to see clearly with our inner eye, be it in powerful images or firm sensations.

As for the Exus and Pomba Giras, the first steps can be as simple as throwing a white sheet over yourself as someone is singing various *pontos*, and in truth if you are playing *pontos* on your sound system after activating the *firmeza* that is also perfectly fine. Light a white candle in front of you.

Doing this you will feel shivers, sensations, laughter and a great variety of other impressions. Try to pay attention to which spirits and what *pontos* cause resonance, and even better let yourself go with the flow as an assistant is taking notes.

This first step is important, because the more agile you get in making distinctions between all these vibrations, the easier will it be to make sense of possessions proper.

Speaking of proper possessions, there are a great variety of these, and it is important to be honest about the stages we are going through, because this is a gradual process. Naturally, spirit possession can be direct and violent, but we sort of want to avoid this in the context of this course, and rather build slowly the mediumistic sensibility.

So, after some time with the white cloth over your head and body you will start doing the same, just with eyes closed, and invite the spirit in. At this stage you will have a bottle of cachaça at your foot and constantly feed the ground where a candle is lit, and avoid drinking yourself. Tobacco can be smoked, but in this case avoid inhaling and fill the air around you with fumes instead. This practice will invite in strange thoughts you know are not your own, and you will feel the mind getting foggy and a different kind of wish to action start to seep in. All this is well and good, and at some point you will take a sip of the *cachaça* and inhale a bit of the cigar, but by gradual, slow steps so you can get familiar with how the spirit enters; also, doing this you ensure that possessions will be more gentle.

Many aspiring mediums that are receiving their Exu/Pomba Gira can get too arrogant in their reception, and this point is important, because after allowing a spirit to take its place in your being there will usually be two voices present, your own and the voice of the spirit, and it is important to know what is what. Only honest practice helps in differentiating one from the other.

The goal should be a genuine two-headed possession, where you are conscious of what is going on, but not really capable of interfering with what the spirit is doing or saying. It is like you are watching yourself from within some place at the back of your head. A lower level of this, but also perfectly good, is when you feel a weight on your shoulders and can truly hear the spirit speaking to you. This is usually called an *encosto*, often in negative ways, but for the medium this is a desirable state. You say and act as the spirit wants you to, but you are still in a great communion. The spirit will drink and smoke through you in this phase, and sometimes the spirit will take advantage of this and intoxicate you so much that a full takeover is made, but this is all a part of the journey and we should not have any fear for this. Rather, such instances will teach us how to mediate the intake of 'spirit food' to indulge this fine balance.

Another modality that can be used to facilitate and train possession is to give *eque*. This means to act as if, to put on a show, to fake it until you make it. There is nothing wrong with this, because acting as if the spirit were present will in many instances attract the spirit, and as the *eque* is performed the spirit will start to enter the game. As said, this can be a good exercise, but it is also important to be honest about what is going on; we want to do things in a way that is genuine and authentic, because the goal of training our mediumship is to become linked to our spirits at all times so they can give us the gift of clairvoyance and true prophecy and fortune telling.

Chapter Eight
A Quimbanda Cosmology

Ganga êh, lê, lê, Ganga êh, lá, lá
Ganga êh, lê, lê, Ganga êh, lá, lá
Gira com Ganga é malelê
Twirling with Ganga is malelê
Exu Tira Teima é mojubá
Exu Easygoing is mojubá

In the arsenal of Quimbanda spells and workings we find an emphasis on using planetary days for given operations. This is a legacy of the ecclesiastical calendar as much as it is a continuation of the folk wisdom of peasants and cunning men and women (*benzedeiras*), who in turn took it from the astrological almanacs popular in the seventeenth and eighteenth centuries in Iberia (and Europe at large for that matter) and were brought to Brazil with trade and travel.

Speaking of the astrological lore amongst the Kimbundu- and Bantu-speaking peoples, little of this was transmitted, it seems, but it is easy enough to recover and, in many ways, even tacitly, Quimbanda does reflect this greater mystery whereby a world that is born must also die, and this is as true for planets as it is for plants. The Congolese Dr. Fu-Kiau explains this in greater detail in his book *African Cosmology of the Bântu-Kôngo*, which sheds light on the metaphysical dimensions that are also of importance for better understanding the roots of Quimbanda. Kongo cosmology is based on the Dikenga (which means to turn or swirl, or in Portuguese 'gira') or Yowa cosmogram, also known as the Kongo Cross, replicatedon the following page. The Yowa Cross represents the cyclical rhythm of all lifeforms, and shows how everything born to a life in the Nseke or world under the Sun must return to Mpemba, the world of the ancestors.

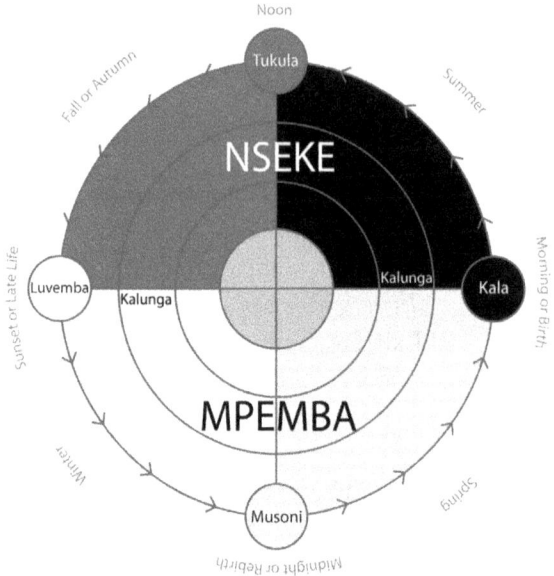

Everything begins as a newborn Sun at Musoni, which indicates the beginning of time or a cycle that begins in the realm of the ancestors, and then we are brought into Kala, or birth, leading us to Tukala, the midday of light associated with creative unfolding and release of our potential as a Sun until we prepare our return at Luvemba, where one ideally is in possession of ndoki/kindoki, 'great powerful wisdom'. We transit from this world and re-enter the abysmal waters where we join again the ancestors and all other spirit hosts. The visible and invisible world are separated by Calunga, which is translated as 'threshold' or 'crossing' and is the metaphysical division between the visible and invisible realm in Quimbanda, associated with the visible field of the cemetery and the mirror of the ocean. In all phases of this cycle *nkisi* is vital. *Nkisi*, or in plural *minkisi*, means 'divine medicine' and can take the shape of any power vested in an object perceived to possess a specific power. The Nganga is the one who manipulates and makes cunning use of the various *minkisi*. *Nganga* means healer in the broader sense of a ritual specialist. Fu-Kiau says of *nkisi* the following:

Man's life attention, ku nseke, is centred on the n'kisi which is the central and most important element in that world. It is the force-element that has power to "kînsa", root-word of n'kisi, meaning to take care, to cure, to heal, to guide by all means even by ceremony. The n'kisi takes care of human beings in all his aspects of life in the world because he has a material body that needs care by n'kisi (medicine). Because he lives in a world surrounded by matadi (M), minerals, bimbenina (B), plants, and bulu (b), animals, his n'kisi (N) must be made of compounds from M-B-b.[11]

The memory of these considerations is still very much at play in Quimbanda, and in particular when it comes to Exu and Pomba Gira who, as tutelary spirit guides, do actively work within this cosmogram as teachers, as forces from the Mpemba that can guide us towards becoming solar beings that over the span of life accumulate *ndoki*, great power that reveals itself in wisdom.

It still remains that Quimbanda, even resting on Bantu bones and lore, is in truth a Brazilian cult, which in so many ways continued the energy and direction of the Bantu legacy, which is one of pragmatic adaptability. We see this from the Bantu cosmology that is occupied with things on earth that hold power, tied to the Ngola proverb: 'The Sun makes God to appear, the earth explains him.' It is in proverbs like this we find the sorcerous attitude active, and this pragmatism makes it difficult for many Westerners to understand the intense fluidity inherent in Quimbanda because it can only be fully understood by establishing a genuine and good connection with a spirit.

We have earlier spoken about how St. Michael, due to what he represents and the qualities he holds, can be seen to represent the Sun. The Sun is such an important symbol and phenomenon, a creator and destroyer in its own right. And while some people get frustrated and irritated with the presence of saints in a cult that they want to be Satanic, not realizing that Satanism is only

---

11 1980: p. 37.

possible as a Christian faction or denomination, we shall try to enter into the primitive mindset, which is concerned with seeing and understanding the presence of power.

The seven traditional planets and their virtues have been with mankind since its dawn, not only in Mesopotamia, Harran, Egypt and Babylon, but all traditional cultures have reverence for the planets and the stellar bodies. The Dogon in northern West Africa have a complex astrological lore tied to their beliefs and magic, as every tribal nation in Africa carries to some extent remnants of a lore tied into the planets and taking omens and prophecy from stellar bodies.

We shall not go too much into detail in these matters, but rather follow the transition of thought still active in Quimbanda and focus on the legacy we are left with.

This legacy tells us that Monday, ruled by the Moon, is a good day to work with Pomba Gira, that Tuesday, the day of Mars, is good for doing works of aggressive magic. Friday is good for Exu and Pomba Gira both, and a day good for love bindings and giving *padê* and offerings, as Saturday is a day good for the Exus and *despachos*.

If we stretch this list and invite in Thursday and Jupiter we find this to be a good day for working favours and doing works involving court and justice. Wednesday, ruled by Mercury, would then be good for communication, trade and all forms of interactions, but also, in truth, given the mercurial element surrounding the Exus, it would be a good night to work these spirits. Sunday, being the ecclesiastical 'day of rest' and going to Mass, would then be a day important for Omolu, Exu Meia-Noite, Exu Quebra-Galho and all other Exus that had a heretic foot in the Church. Also, some deem Sunday good for healing, as it is a day when the miracle of the Eucharist is enacted.

My point in presenting this is about the pragmatic use of knowledge, which is distinctively Bantu or Kongo. We see this in how many Congo prophets since the sixteenth century could experience something powerful and overwhelming related to the crucifix or some saint, and gave to this experience a completely different, personal—yet cosmic—dimension that involved and yet exceeded the content of meaning and story in a saint or a relic.

Personally I believe this Kongolese attitude is replicated in how so many of the Exus and Pomba Giras have multiple incarnations, avenues of invitation to a given mystery that can be breached from a variety of angles, simply because any extraordinary life mimics the life of a saint by being memorable, and thus we find that linear time is not any longer dealing the cards or setting the rules, we are moving around in magical time sequences, just like the feast day of a saint is celebrated every year as if that saint were present on that day, in spite of having been dead for hundreds of years. The celebration of memory brings the past into the present, but in a different way. If we look at a King Exu like Exu Mor that is from before the beginning of time, and yet had multiple manifestations in various forms, we can get an idea of the complexity involved in the power a given Exu might represent.

So, seeing Quimbanda from within this cosmic dimension that goes back to the beginning of time, as powers rooted in original and rustic principles of protective being that had multiple incarnations, we see a landscape taking shape that is of immense proportions. It might be that it is because of this sheer extension, and lack of discrimination and condemnation, caused by this richness of experience we find, that Quimbanda embraces what is considered fringe, heretical, bad and depraved as much as it embraces love, kindness, generosity and the sublime.

Yet, it is the people of the street, the hustlers, heretics, outlaws, and prostitutes we find taking precedence in the realm of Quimbanda. The Umbandist explanation and solution is that these are spirits void of light that should be brought into serving an Orixá so they can grow in light.

The Quimbandeiro, however, will view our spirits very differently; our Exus and Pomba Giras are brimful with light—but also they are storehouses of human experience and knowledge, which enables them to understand the human condition in all its aspects. In presenting themselves as hustlers and whores, heretics and outlaws, they challenge us and our moral code as much as they manifest an absence of judgment about our flaws. Rather, they represent a message that tells us that we can overcome and become exalted in what we are; it is all about acceptance and refraining from judgment.

Hence it becomes important to stress that when Zélio made Umbanda in 1908, he had previous and continuous experience with the spirits that were worked in the houses of macumba in Rio, and he invited them in, because Zélio did not believe in judging anyone, yet he saw in inviting in these spirits an opportunity to bring them to the light, which is perhaps a judgment in its own right?

Anyway, what appears to us is that the Exus and Pomba Giras of Quimbanda hold their own light, they don't need to be placed under the slavery of Orixás or saints to be elevated. The one that makes the elevation is the practitioner himself, and this elevation is not about bringing a dark spirit to light but about a greater cosmic harmony where the understanding of the human condition and a sense of power is developed.

Certainly, working with spirits who have accepted and embraced the shadow of the human condition brings challenges in its own right. For instance, a person that has as his guide Exu dos Infernos can be tempted to follow a similar path as this Exu had in his incarnations, which is one of hustling and dealing, ending in misery and death. This is an error; remember, these spirits come as teachers accepting good and bad, and thus their errors made in their incarnations are not what they seek to pass on, but the lesson of a life lived like that. This is not about bringing something from darkness to light, but bringing the light of clarity to a relationship.

The same can be said about disincarnated spirits that turn into vampire spirits; the Calunga Pequena are full of these life-thirsty beings, and we have a Queen Pomba Gira that takes care of them. This should speak loud and clear to us about how not to give in to temptations, but rather strive to understand and control what we are so we can effectuate our essence in a diligent and firm manner, like for instance Exu Morcego.

Malandragem, or hustling, is another important aspect of Quimbanda, clearly an inheritance from the macumba houses in Rio that developed hustling into an art form, embodied by Zé Pelintra. But we need to understand that this celebration of '*malandragem*' was not about petty crimes and the acts of lowlifes. On the contrary, it was about being street-smart, but also a somewhat learned gentleman. The many stories about Zé Pelintra speak of a man who studied medicine and law, but choose to stay in the lousy taverns interacting with common people, gambling and defending women from abuse. In this way, good old Zé typifies the perfection of the Quimbandeiro, a person who knows his tricks and games, who knows what he knows but also realizes that the people of the street, of the cemetery, woods, and crossroads, make up the human experience, which is an experience of the divinity in itself.

Some of our beloved spirits are full of anger and bitterness, they want to drink and smoke too much. Not because they are evil, but because they look for that harmony a king or queen can give to a wayward knight or dame. In this the responsibility of the Quimbandeiro lays heavy and hard in finding that balance between everything, replacing judgment with understanding. Because if we do this, we will notice power wherever it might be and take advantage of it, the greatest advantage always being to grow a little bit wiser in both realms.

Chapter Nine
How to Understand Exu

Ele é um anjo que caiu do céu
He is an angel who fell from the Heaven
Ele não é homem, ele não é mulher
He is not man, he is not woman
Ele é do dia, ele é da noite
He is the Day, He is the Night
Que Anjo é esse, é seu Lúcifer
What angel is this, it is Mr. Lucifer

✦✦✦✦✦✦✦✦✦✦✦✦

De onde vem Exu Caveira
Exu Caveira come from where
De onde vem o Senhor do Cemitério
Lord of the Cemetery come from where
Mas ele vem zoando, zoando
But, he comes joking and laughing
Pra quebrar toda a demanda
To break every negativity
Exu Caveira vem chegando
Exu Skull comes arriving

There are many opinions about who Exu is. If we look at the ideas found in contemporary Brazil about who he is, we find that the sentiments and ideas vary greatly. with some embracing the concept of Orixá Èṣú, i.e., that Quimbanda Exu is a trickster living at the crossroad. Given that Ifá says he is the youngest of Orixá, some have infused the idea that Èṣú is the slave of Orixá, and thus this have been imposed on the Quimbanda Exu and explained in a Kardecist/Umbandist frame of mind. But before we go there, let us clarify that the Orixá Èṣú was never a slave of anyone, he is the friend of Orunmila (the spirit of Wisdom), Ogun (the spirit of iron and fire) and Obatala (the spirit of whiteness, purity and dreams) in particular, and was assigned the responsibility of transmitting *àsé*, or transformative power, to the world and bringing sacrifices and prayers to the creator spirit, Olodumare. If we look at the Quimbanda Exu we find some of these features transposed upon him, with some alterations. We find wisdom gained through living life in pursuit of 'the edge', what is in general dubbed *malandragem*, or hustling, but it is important to be precise in the use of this term as we have several candidates surfacing in English. A *malandro* is a scoundrel, a hustler, but it is not the insidious kind of hustler; it is more the cunning and crafty one. He is foxy more than tricky and he has a code. This code is intimately related to his word, as his word is his bond, and it also means that with Exu you get what you expect, which should be logical given his cunning and crafty essential nature. So for Exu to hold himself up as a mirror for he or she who calls or summons him is no big feat, it comes easy, naturally, almost effortlessly. This adaptability of Exu is most interesting and it is this mercurial essence that has enabled these spirits or entities to shape the parts of Orixá, departed spirits, renegade saints and fallen angels into this bohemian streetwise entity whose seven principal attributes are the laughter, the crossroad, the cemetery, the night, the pepper, the booze and the cigar.

In the same way as Exu rose from all these attributes to be unique and distinct, we also see the same patchwork, if you will, at play in his cult. We can see this in the fusion of words, for instance *cainana*, like in the *ponto* that goes like this:

> Exu Cainana, quem te matou, Cainana\Exu Cainana, quem te matou, Cainana\Foi Seu Marabô\Cainana\ Foi Exu Veludo\Cainana\Foi Exu do Lodo\Cainana\ quem te matou.

Viper Exu\Who killed the viper\Viper Exu, who killed the viper\It was Mr. Marabô\Viper\It was Exu Velvet\Viper\It was Exu of the Mud\Viper\Who killed you.

Cainana is a Bantu term for viper, as Quimbanda is an Angolan word and Ganga is a Bantu word and the frequently used '*mojubá*' is a Yoruba word. The same goes for the *padê*, a dish of cassava or corn flour mixed with peppers and palm oil that is offered to Exu and Pomba Gira, which is a fusion of the Yoruba sacramental (and common) food *ekó*, a polenta that serves as food for men and spirits alike, and the Brazilian *farofa*, that does the same—which happened to come to Brazil in the trans-Atlantic crossing, most likely from the coast of Mina, which would suggest a Bantu-Kongo origin. Exu is a pragmatic spirit and his cult is equally pragmatic.

As said, there are many ideas around concerning the true nature of Exu, but let us get rid of those most biased by Christian moralism and Manichaeism, namely that Exu is like the demons subordinated to angels as a controlling or consenting force. This idea has led to the common belief that Exu is the slave of Orixá and equally controlled by *caboclos* and *pretos-velhos*. That Exu can conform to such classification is obviously within his capacity, but that an amoral spirit like Exu would do so because he is forced, not because this is his place, is doubtful. He will accept such a place amidst other spirits for some reason other than spiritual demand and repercussion. In the Quimbanda in the south of Brazil (Quimbanda de Cruzeiro e Almas) Exu is seen as a free agent, not subordinated to anyone outside of what might be the hierarchy in the legion of Quimbanda of which he makes himself a part. In this particular perception, this was caused by a deliberate spiritual action known as *cruzamento*, a ritual fusion between the Orixá Èṣú and the Quimbanda Exu, which had the purpose of giving Exu his freedom from spiritual tyranny.

Another idea is the one concerning the transitions of Exu, or maturation from 'pagan' to 'baptized' to 'crowned', which in the literature of Umbanda frequently is seen as the natural process of indoctrinating, educating or taming Exu, where gaining a crown also entails that he has managed to turn away from his wicked ways and side with Jesus Christ, as if there ever was an inherent conflict between Exu and Jesus Christ. The other way of seeing this triple transition is that Exu learns through trance, mediumship and spirit work to act with more agility in our material world, hence a crowned Exu is an Exu that can speak and interact with people, and his crown is more a symbol of his dominance and functionality in our material world than anything else.

This force we call Exu is amoral, it is a force of fire and death that holds the memory of human life and living. In this, Exu challenges us by dragging out our weaknesses and displaying shamelessly his own depravity in carefree acceptance of all the variety we find in human life. Exu doesn't judge, but is also a mirror for us, and in this he challenges. Can you leave judgment alone? Can you accept yourself warts and all? Can you leave be the shithead next door as you focus on your own pleasure?

Not only this, but we have so many accounts where Exu speaks of his past incarnations, in whatever guise, that are always about being punished for his good deeds or getting the full avalanche of misery due to his bad deeds, often intertwined as exemplified by Zé Pelintra, who met his death defending a woman who had defended him earlier. Exu Meia-Noite can tell stories of the heresy committed in his incarnations as a priest, heresy always perpetrated to help someone or to seek greater understanding. Every Exu represents a transgressive and socially antinomian dilemma playing itself out in this field of moral and social obedience turning into shit, death and memory.

The greater notion of Exus is therefore that they are *mortos* or souls of departed people, they are revenants and the spirits of people who lived lives typical for a given Exu, returning as friends, teachers and challengers of the living. I do agree with this notion, but we also have to keep in mind that what we call 'Exu' is denominating an energetic field related to places of power from the beginning of time. Hence the returning dead are entering into harmony with this field of noetic activity, and because of this harmony we can recognize what we know as Exus.

The presence of the dead souls is what generates the legions around the prime forms of the various Exus. This prime force that attracts a given stratum or type of *mortos* is a cosmic principle, as should be evident in the presence of Exu Lucifer, often called 'King of Quimbanda', hence there is present in Quimbanda the idea of the fall of the angelic host, and it might be because of this common origin that the demonic offspring of the fallen host and the demonic features of Exu find a meeting point in diabolic iconography. Yet, they are still spirits moved by the same pull that caused the fall of the angelic host, material life, which in the case of the fallen angels was concerned with the erotic, as they sought out the daughters of Cain to both enjoy and have children with. In the case of Exu, it is about the plethora of hedonist enjoyment, strong emotions and vivid sentiments and experiences, to be present in the fire of life.

So with this notion in place, we can conclude that the Exus that are attracted to us are attracted because they sense a harmony, an affinity with us, and if we allow it they can enter our lives as teachers and friends. We have in this also the notion of Exu being a troublemaker, and a punitive one as such. And this is true, this spirit can bring disaster, and at times in no small scale. So how to understand this?

We already addressed his virtue and nature being fiery and amoral—and so what are we dealing with as the premise for interaction? Why do some people have problems mastering the influence of Exu in their lives?

It is rooted in harmony and attitude. There is perhaps not much that is moral in the realms of Exu, but we have codes for everything and these codes are always somewhat polite. For instance, when we start our session at the *tronco* we knock three times on the floor either with our left hand or left foot; if we have a room or house reserved for him, we knock three times on the door and address him as *Seu* Exu (Mr. Exu), in reverence and respect. And from these first gestures we need to follow up the code in our workings and our *'demandas'*. For instance, a person who makes a working to kill someone, his success depends on a variety of issues, one being how unprotected his target is. Another issue is what this person gives the Exu to work with— I mean a simple *farofa* and a *Contra-filé* is not really fuel to commit murder. But the third element is perhaps more important than any other, namely your bearing, your attitude. In the case of asking Exu for murder, you need to be able to go through with the act yourself; only a murderer at heart can demand murder from his friend, because these spirits will not really listen to a coward's plea. They need to respect you and feel this bond you have is worthy of what you ask. It is a road of mutual speed and interaction that rests in mutual respect, and it is this mutual respect which I find lies in your Exu being crowned.

Certainly, Exu can challenge you and place you in awkward situations just because he thinks it is good for you, to stimulate your own 'crowning'. But the more we appraise this relationship as one bound by this code of honour and harmony it seems to circle around, the better our work will be.

We might think of Exu as an older friend, a friend that doesn't care for your safety, but for your crown. He cares about the code between the two of you and the worth you give him—and yourself. This is something replicated in never giving to Exu what you don't like yourself. This doesn't mean that you should make yourself poor in pleasing your friend, but that you should offer things you like yourself. Some people have an attitude that any greasy booze or cheap cigar is good enough for Exu—they themselves would never drink or smoke it, but for the spirit it is good enough. This might not generate a functional bond with spirit as here we establish a dissonance between what we offer and what we expect. It is good to remember that Exu and Pomba Gira are mostly people, like you and me, that take shape in flesh, fire, tobacco, and booze, hence for the most part what takes place in human interactions and relationships can very well be used as analogies for how we interact with Exu and Pomba Gira. Abusive and dysfunctional patterns, if allowed to play out between humans or between human and spirit, are equally devastating. Now, if you give what you can, and what you can is of a lesser quality than what you would want because you are poor, this is another story—this is about sacrifice, yet another code in the interaction with and understanding of Exu.

So no matter the legacy involved, of which we have been speaking and will be speaking more of, Exu represents this man at the border of society, the man who has become amoral due to the lessons of his life. Yet there is the code of respect and honour everywhere, as much as there is laughter at our depravities and shortcomings, and finding ways to achieve our goals.

Exu is a composite of fire and Saturn, tobacco, hard liquor and flaming coals, and in offering up these things we attract him and enable him to stay. It is by the same means we invite him into our body, by tobacco fumes and booze and the power of peppers in whatever form they are presented, be it by energy and mode or in presenting the actual peppers.

We see in how the Exus revel in the pleasures of human life how these offerings stimulate their memory and presence, and how this makes them come alive for a moment to speak, share and give counsel, as past brothers of living humanity, who learned from their mistakes and good deeds and are more than willing to stay with us and share these memories and help us in our own journey.

This is why we find Exus everywhere, especially at any form of crossroad. These are places of choices, and choices are at the heart of the human experience, and they are also guardians of the life lived in extraordinary ways.

CHAPTER TEN

How to Understand Pomba Gira

> Boa noite pra quem é da noite
> *Good night to whom is of the night*
> Boa noite pra quem vem chegando
> *Good night to whom just arrived*
> Boa noite pra moça bonita
> *Good night to the beautiful lady*
> É pra ela que estamos cantando
> *It is for her we are singing*

It seems that the spirit we know as Pomba Gira is derived from the Kongolese spirit Mbumba Nzila/Pambujila which I have translated previously as 'the erotic snake at the crossroad', Mbumba signifying the snake and Nzila meaning crossroad or crossing. I believe we are here speaking of the Bantu concept of *kisimbi*, which are snake spirits tied to nature and ancestry that are focused on multiplication and fertility, and in themselves also hold the memory of earth and time. While the Angolan serpentine spirits known as Pambujila appear to have been the point of origin for the solidification of the Pomba Giras and Exus in tune with the pulse of Quimbanda, the most famous of the Pomba Giras, often referred to as the Queen of Quimbanda, Maria Padilha, was a historical person. The historical Maria Padilha was named Maria Padilla and was born in 1334. At the age of nineteen she became the lover of King Pedro I of Castile in Spain. Her myth tells that she married the king in secrecy in 1353, the same year he married the French princess of Bourbon, leaving Maria Padilla to become a queen without a crown. Maria Padilla died in 1361, only twenty-seven years old, and was buried three times. First, she was buried in the Monastery of Santa Clara, the construction and inauguration of which Maria Padilla herself had officiated.

In 1362, however, Pedro officially pronounced his marriage with Maria Padilla and had his marriage to the princess of Bourbon annulled, hence the remains of Maria Padilla were moved to the Cathedral of Seville, where upon the death of Pedro she was again moved to rest with the remains of her king in their crypt. And then we find something curious in the notes from an *auto da fé* of the Inquisition of Lisbon, from the year 1640, where Maria Padilla is conjured by the accused witch, as we can read here:

> I conjure thee vinegar, pepper and sulphur in name of so and so, with three from the bakery, three from the cutlery, three form the butchery, three from the yard, three from the weighting, all three. All six, all nine will gather in the heart of so and so, if they are more, or if they are less, 56 devils will gather, in the tower of Primão they will climb nine rods for love they will fetch, in the millstone of Caiphas they will sharpen, in the heart of so and so they will pierce, so he cannot be, or be at rest, until he be with me; Dona Maria de Padilla with all your squad bring me so and so through the air and by the winds; Marta the lost who for the love of a man went to hell, so I ask that you partake of your love with so and so, so he cannot sleep, nor has rest, until he is with me.[12]

Clearly in the years after her death she took on distinctive sorcerous features, and there are two elements of consideration that can explain this. One is that Castile was neighbour to Navarre and the Alpine regions of Spain and France where we find Basque land, hence Maria Padilla was living in the vicinity where Pierre de Lancre in 1609 made his investigation on behalf of the Inquisition to clean this region of heresy and witchcraft. The second is that Castile was a place quite livid with 'alternative theologies', and of those in particular the *alumbrados*, a short-lived sect from 1510, are interesting to mention. The *alumbrados* or 'Illuminated' were led by female spiritual leaders, called *beatas*,

---

12 In Maggi, Humberto & Rivas, Veronica, 2015: p. 10.

and enjoyed the support of Castile's Cardinal Cisneros until 1524 when two of their leaders came before the Tribunal of Toledo and were condemned for heresy. They considered external rituals not only useless, but as chains and weights, ties to the material world that would only hinder one's abandonment to God. Not only that, but their use of meditation to achieve states of divine mania, a state beyond good and evil where the sacred became erotic, sensual and coloured by eros and desire, didn't fall on good soil with the tribunal in Toledo either. Of interest to our timeline is the fact that even if the sect itself didn't last long, its reputation was far from short-lived, and *alumbrados* became in the seventeenth century associated with both mystical and physical eroticism, as María Tausiet recounts:

> With regard to the importance of physical contact among the "Valencian *alumbrados*," there are many examples of what Huerga has termed the "pornographic phase of the sect," which began in the late years of the seventeenth century in the Extremadura region. According to him, many "women, deranged by several unscrupulous clerics, went with fanatical fervour [...] from the ecstasy of mystic quietism to an open sexual one," so that "the austere life of Extremadura's countryside was turned into an unbridled bacchanalia.[13]

In the practice of Quimbanda today we can see how this prime idea of the Kongolese erotic serpent crosses over to our world and takes shape in myriad forms, Maria Padilha being one of several proper shades of this triumphant force. In this transition alone we find folk magic and sorcery also crossing over, fusing Bantu sorcery with continental cunning arts. Maria Padilha became associated with the witch, the free woman, the heretic, the rebellion and of course the whore. And let us stay a bit with Pomba Gira the harlot. Naturally, this sobriquet 'whore' plays back upon being a king's lover, an uncrowned queen, as much as

---

13 2020: p. 314.

a libertine woman in no need of a man, another definition of the prostitute. Of interest in this regard is that in Brazil there was a law that was actively upheld from 1934 to 1964 that relegated the practice of macumba to be dealt with by the same department that was responsible for dealing with prostitution, gambling, and alcohol and other drugs, a most proper environment for Pomba Gira to flourish in all her beautifully shameless and challenging erotic presence. Whilst Exu challenges us on our word, loyalty and fabricated morals, Pomba Gira challenges us on our prejudice, our shame and our capacity for truthfulness and honesty.

We have several examples of how Pomba Gira plays herself out as a literary theme, and amongst the better ones might be Jorge Amado's book *Gabriela, Cravo e Canela* (1958), which can be said to give life to the ideal form of Pomba Gira in the ways of the libertine Gabriela. And it is also from the 50s and 60s that we find Pomba Giras rising in strength and presence, not due to Amado's celebration of the strong and free woman, but because the times were a-changing, making her form become pregnant with power in that era. Hence the motif of the free woman is perhaps a continuation of the celebration of the *carioca malandro* invested in strong and independent women.

As such it is important to understand Pomba Gira in a social context of women's liberation and, conversely, the suppression of women. In Bantu cultures, women were never suppressed as they were in the Brazilian culture, rather woman was always seen as a natural vessel for the witchcraft powers; not only this, but the miracle of giving new life always placed woman in a position of awe and mystery. Hence, the discontinuity between Bantu concepts and what we find in Brazil is so great that we are better off understanding Pomba Gira in the Iberian and Brazilian continuum than the African.

When we look at the varieties of Pomba Giras, we find them amongst the nomads, at the beaches, amongst the stars, in the cemeteries and in the woods. They are always sensual and/or provocative. For instance, most Queens tend to challenge us, while those without a crown try to tempt us into accepting the challenges they represent. Some of them are nymphs with a touch of vampirism; others are more crone-like, as in the case of the Queen of the Calunga, who does have legions of nymph-like Pomba Giras under her dress, but herself has become wise and kind since her own nymph-like past.

We have in Brazil the expression 'to have Pomba Gira in front', which amongst several interpretations also means that your Pomba Gira is what people notice first, and not you. This is usually considered an impediment, as having Pomba Gira in the front can lead to sensual and abusive attention from males. Certainly, when this happens it is due to Pomba Gira training the woman she walks ahead of to stand up for herself, but also presenting options that can be rejected or accepted. The bad reputation given to having her in front is due to the chauvinism and demands for heteronormative masculinity we find in Latin cultures like Brazil, that when fused with the push towards freedom and desire forged by Pomba Gira can at times become a complex issue. Pomba Gira is the Queen supreme of Quimbanda. We find references to this in several *pontos* that speak about 'how we shake the Fig Tree to see which Exu falls', and the *ponto* speaking of Pomba Gira as the woman of seven husbands, celebrating her triumphant role as an independent woman that is in control of her life.

Due to this, Pomba Gira equally willingly dresses in the role of a prostitute and seductress as she does in the robe of comforter of souls, and in this we realize that successfully working with Pomba Gira is truly about your constitution.

For instance, a woman that succumbs to abuse in spite of petitions to Dona Pomba Gira to help her is one not yet able to make use of the force given to her, and will tend to be subject to challenges, because Pomba Gira helps in giving power and means to solve your abused condition, and she keeps on doing this until you embrace the strength.

What we see is that Pomba Gira is truly an ally of women in general. Her aim is to liberate woman and make her strong. It so follows that men working with her need to watch their ways with women. A batterer of women, someone who looks down on women or patronizes them, tends to be in danger of offending Pomba Gira herself. This means that women have a natural access to the aid of her forces, which would be in harmony with the Bantu idea of this force, while men should approach with some care. And in this let me present an example.

Works done with Pomba Gira aimed towards love and reconciliation, finding love and sensual delights, are usually easy works, but sometimes nothing happens—and there is always a reason for it. Sometimes the person wanting the work is obsessed with someone who don't want her or him and thus it makes things difficult, and we may question if we should even waste time and good candles on such endeavours. Another situation is this man that came to me some years back wanting to be reunited with his wife. We made a working and it was unsuccessful. He came back and we made another working, and this time his wife actually called him and wanted to speak. He went there to speak with her, she set down some boundaries and he ended up beating her. He came back for the third time and told me that 'he snapped'. I asked if this was the first time 'he snapped', but no, it turned out that his beating and abuse of his wife was what made her leave him. Such cases are then closed down and there is nothing that should be done to bind the couple together. Yet the working demonstrated how Pomba Gira enticed this bond and brought them together… so a final hard lesson could be given in order for the woman to accept herself and end the abuse. And so, if you are male and an abuser of women or find them to be inferior, you should perhaps tread very, very carefully with these spirits.

At the root of Quimbanda we find the Queen of the Fig Tree in Hell, or simply Pomba Gira do Inferno, Pomba Gira of Hell synthesised with Astaroth. There is little spoken of her in Brazil simply because she represents the pure, untamed power of woman, the kind of woman that holds seven husbands in her harem and binds herself to none but herself. The Queen of Seven Crossroads is a form of her that is more tangible for us, but we find again the same mystery playing itself out, the one of woman being in charge.

An example from my own early practice might illustrate this well: enthusiastic with having managed to seat my Exus and Pomba Gira, I was looking forward to deepening the relationship. But a force was always denying me permission to speak with my spirits unless I gave her due respect, tribute, and offerings—and that I spoke Portuguese. It was a humbling year, but I listened to her and I followed her demands. This first troublesome year proved to be of great worth and value; standing strong in her tests of my motivation and character enabled me to gain some sort of good will from the Queen of Seven Crossroads. The impact was so great that I will actually advise anyone to start working with their Pomba Gira, because in truth she is the root and key of Quimbanda. For males this reflects in our attitude towards women in general, and over time it turns into a dual flow where the way we treat and understand women is also in tune with the benefits we are gaining from Pomba Gira.

Women have everything to gain from cultivating their Pomba Gira, but should also be aware of how Pomba Gira seeks her daughter's strength, independence, and self-secure attitude as a fulfilled woman.

As we see, Pomba Gira is a force that cultivates values and attitudes. While Exu is bound by some code of honour, Pomba Gira is about respect, independence, and more than everything, absence of judgment.

From this we can perhaps interpret Quimbanda as a cult of chivalry when we look closer at the nature of the spirits we are working with. Sure they curse, swear, challenge as they drink and smoke. But the tobacco, perfumes, drinks, and food are all things that attract them towards the place of veneration, and the fumes and essences of these offerings of earth they use to embody themselves for a little time. Hence, as any chthonic spirit, they can come alive for some time by being offered fumes, virtues, and essences of earth to simply 'earth' them.

CHAPTER ELEVEN
The Realm of Quimbanda

> Sete facas de ponta em cima de uma mesa
> *Seven blades upon the table*
> sete velas acesas lá na encruzilhada
> *seven candles blazing in the crossroad*
> o exu é rei alupande[14] o exu é rei alupande
> *Exu is king oh yeah! Exu is king oh yeah!*
> o exu é rei lá nas sete encruzilhadas
> *Exu is king in the seven crossroads*

Quimbanda is a necromantic cult, and also a sorcerous cult that has chronically been labelled as 'black magic' and 'low spiritism'. Since the 1950s the 'goetic' dimension has also entered by virtue of several of the demons from *Grimorium Verum* being syncretized with the Exus, and indeed Quimbanda is as goetic as it is chthonic and telluric. But one must understand that 'goetic' does not refer to summoning the goetic demons from the *Lemegeton*, but to the fine line between life and death, as Frater Acher summarizes:

> ...the primal sorcery of the first goêtes: to establish and maintain boundaries between the realm of the dead and the living, to uphold the threshold between the chthonic and the human world. Equally they were the forces through which human priests would also cross these thresholds – and interact with forces and beings from the

---

14 *Alupande* is a greeting used by Exu Sete Encruzilhadas to salute his friends and compatriots.

other side. The Idaian Dactyls[15] all in one represented the door, the key, and the threshold as well as the guardians who watched over it.[16]

    This precise definition of goetic work is in complete harmony with the essence of Quimbanda, as here we do cross over to the other side and also allow for spirits to constantly cross over to our side, hence the meeting between Tata and Exu is yet again a crossroad of power maintaining the threshold intact. Further, the label 'black magic' is also a proper one, but we must see this in the right context. Black magic derived from *nigromancia*, which became necromancy in its more modern Latinised form in the 1600s, hence we experienced a transition from the more all-encompassing 'black arts' (*nigromancia*) to 'divination by the dead' (necromancy) in particular. These 'black arts' were the disciplines of natural philosophy that set out to explain the mysteries of blackness: the night, the earth or the chthonic darkness hidden within the earth. The *mantik* or divinatory importance is also vital to take notice of, as the oracular process is integral to Quimbanda as well where the medium possessed by the spirit can be asked questions and give answers as much as a spirit through the human vessel can effectuate magical workings and give counsel on how to perform magical workings and processes for a variety of ends.

    Quimbanda is also worked at night with spirits and entities that thrive upon night, stars and the moon, and adding its African legacy, its black roots from Angola, Kongo and other parts of West Africa, we gain a complete *nigromantic* world that has been interwoven at least since the 1850s and the arrival of grimoires and the French demonological tradition to Brazil along with French middle class immigrants, in particular to Rio de Janeiro which was the capital from 1822–1960. Adding to this imagery,

---

15 'Idaian Dactyls' refers to the mountain-dwelling servants of Adrasteia, a mountain nymph associated with Rhea herself, that gave birth to a host of male mountain-born daimons/numina in charge of maintaining the threshold between the chthonic realm and the world of the living.
16 2021: p. 30.

Iberian justice since early in the seventeenth century exiled criminals, including people convicted for witchcraft, to Brazil. It appears that these exiled cunning folks contributed to some legacy in Brazil, as already in the early eighteenth century Brazil was taking care of their own witchcraft persecution with a couple of interesting cases that should be mentioned. One concerns an investigation by the Jesuit Manuel da Silva between the years of 1750 and 1758 in the northern state of Piauí that found women involved in sabbath flight, orgies and demonic pacts. In the same period, we find in southeast Brazil, in São Paulo, a woman by the name Ursulina de Jesus being burned for the heresy of witchcraft in 1754. The case against Ursulina was presented by her husband, Sebastião, who claimed his wife had made him infertile by the use of witchcraft. Not long after Ursulina was consumed by the flames, Sebastião married his lover, Cesária, but continued childless. The European legacy in the form of folk Catholicism and *curandeirismo* impacted greatly the magical vision in Brazil and entered Quimbanda through the *pretos-velhos*, seen as wise Old Blacks guarding this knowledge and passing it on to the Exus and Pomba Giras, and sometimes even as Quimbandeiros themselves in the form of *Pretos-Velhos Quimbandeiros*.

In this ingenious and rich cultural and spiritual climate, the outcast ones found one another and made sub-communities and liaisons on their own, bound by their common rejection of the rulers of their world. The macumba of olden days was where the suppressed and weak, the subversive and ostracised went to get their centre in focus, their vengeance executed and their soul healed and anointed by the Devil.

My belief is that all these lines somehow melted and merged in the interaction of practice that was more available in the houses of macumba in Rio after 1888, which after some decades became more unified and similar. At least the accounts given to us by João do Rio in his 1904 work about 'the religions in Rio' at the time would suggest the validity of such hypothesis.

In this regard it is good to have a look at the precursor of macumba, Quimbanda, and Umbanda, namely the *cabula*. This

Kikongo word refers to the drumbeat used to conjure Besseim, the Omolu of Candomblé de Angola, though it has also been said to be a corruption of 'cabala', but perhaps more interesting in this scope is to understand what this practice was about, as here we find the common root of so much Brazilian spirituality. The most complete account of what *cabula* was is given by Dom João Batista Corrêa Nery, who gave a livid account of this practice in 1901, and in the ethnographic writings of the anthropologist Raimundo Nina Rodrigues in his *Os Africanos no Brasil* published in 1906.

Cabula was a fusion of elements Catholic, Spiritist, Bantu, Angolan and also from the Malê. The Malê referred to Africans from Mali and to Islamised peoples like the Hausa and Tapa, but from 1870 until 1920 we find João do Rio writing about the Malê in Rio de Janeiro all dressing in white and wearing the kufi, who were very well versed in sorcery and performed divination with the *opele Ifá*. We find in the *cabula* a synthesis of the spiritual legacy of Brazil radiating out from Bahia, up north to Pernambuco and to the states south and east of Bahia, like Rio de Janeiro, Espírito Santo and Minas Gerais.

The rituals were always done in the woods, in a place called *camucite*, 'secret place' close to a tree of importance for the cult, and a fire was made. Here they prepared tables in the form of tablecloths spread on the ground with candles, images and offerings to Catholic saints, like Santa Bárbara, Santa Maria, and Cosmas and Damian amongst others. The priest officiating the ceremony was called *embanda*, *umbanda* or *Pai de Terreiro* and was assisted by a *cambone*. The people attending were called *mucambos* and *mucambas* and the ritual gathering was called *engiras*. The people gathered were dressed in white and had their heads covered with a bandana or a kufi. The ceremonies were performed by clapping the rhythms by hand and singing *pontos cantados* which were called 'nimbus' to call the *tatás* of the *engira*. These *tatás* had names like Rompe-Mato (Shatterer of Woods), Flor de Carunga (Cemetery-flower), and Arranca-Toco (Stump uprooter), that were received in possession together with the spirits called *santé*, or saint, which were considered the most important spirit guides of each one in the assembly. These *tatás* obviously were *caboclos*, *pretos-velhos* and Exus with a given inclination that we today call Quimbanda.

The *engira* was opened by the following salutation:

Dai-me licença, carunga
Allow me to enter, Calunga
Dai-me licença, tatá
Allow me to enter, Tatá
Dai-me licença, bacúla
Allow me to enter, spirits of death and forest
Que embanda qué quendá
So this chief can turn you from there to here

At this point the *embanda* would chew the root, drink the wine and fumigate the tables with further calls to the *baculo* of the air, saluting the glowing embers used for fumigation and then asking 'to fall' in the *engira*, meaning to be subject to trance and possession by the tutelary spirits. It is also worthy to mention that the *baculo/a* derives from the Kimbundo *bakulo*, which in the first place refers to a powerful ancestor, and in the second place an ancestral spirit that lives in the woods.

We know that as a part of the initiation it was necessary to chew a root, most likely jurema or something else rich in DMT, that was taken with wine. Considering that to this day the bark of the root of the jurema tree is steeped in red wine, this tree might well have been the entheogen used. Markings were made with *emba*, which today is called *pemba*, on various parts of the body.

Cabula gave way to the practice of macumba, and it is especially in the *macumba carioca* that we find a division between Umbanda and Quimbanda; by the 1940s there was a full-fledged right/left dichotomy to be found, where saints and Orixás were seen as forces dominating the spirits of Quimbanda. Perhaps a perspective inherited and continued from the *santidade*, but apparently in the twentieth century the difference between the classes of spirits attending the *engiras*, parted into more evolved (Umbanda) and less evolved (Quimbanda), became a dominant idea.

THE REALM OF QUIMBANDA

Quimbanda is at its core the cult of Exu and Pomba Gira, a chthonic and fiery dynamic between a blazing Saturn and a regal Venus, which became the name adopted by these *tatás* and *baculas* the people of the *cabula* were working in the woods. In applying astrological language in aiding our understanding, we also reveal that Pomba Gira is all things Venusian and Exu is all things fiery and Saturnine, which is replicated in scented cigarillos, the wine, the tobacco, the champagne, the cognac, whiskey and cachaça, the meat, *farofa* and perfume we give to them under candlelight and veil of night. The way the practice is understood to work should speak volumes to us. Quimbanda is about everything that happens in this field between Saturn and Venus cloaked by night. Quimbanda is about a given ray or vibration, a mystery in itself that summons spirits Saturnine and Venusian, spirits of the woods and spirits intertwined with dead souls and chthonic spirits. It is room for the Caboclo Quimbandeiro as it is room for the Preto-Velho Quimbandeiro, mysterious forest spirits of a violent and wise temper, and in this perspective perhaps also cousins from the grammar of *Verum*. Quimbanda has proven itself to be amazingly inclusive both when it comes to types of spirits, and the absence of judgment toward the people who knock on the door to the house of Exu.

It is from this gathering of nocturnal and chthonic spirits that the unique 'liturgy' or code of work of each temple or *terreiro* is made. After all, Quimbanda has no dogmas, as it is completely based upon the doctrine given through the tradition in initiatic situations, but this legacy is transformed in harmony with the tutelary spirits that guide and inform the work. This point is perhaps the most important one to observe, as it is here that so much can go wrong on this fine line between what spirits want and need and what the Tata wants. For instance, when someone speaks of elevating spirits and this holds a material connotation of, for instance, making Exu vegetarian or denying him drink, blood or tobacco, they are not doing Quimbanda and they are not having a spirit connection. Rather they are possessed by their own conviction and want to subdue the spirit to their own tastes and inclinations and preferences. They act as someone who seeks to impose their values upon someone else—and this attitude will never work. In this the host becomes hostile and the spirits will leave, not because of vengeance, but simply due to the fact that the offerings we give to Exu are what enables him to take shape and come close; denying this by simple rejection of bonds makes him become far and distant.

The other element is about the Quimbanda world view. Quimbanda is about seeing power wherever it is, seeking to understand how to use it and, depending on this, inviting it in—or not. Quimbanda offers a way towards connecting with lascivious mermaids and the ocean shore, stern Omolu who commands the dead, and the spirits mingling with beggars and drunkards circling the tavern. Quimbanda is not about rejection, but acceptance. It is the eye of the healer and shaman of the world that sees what is for what it is and neglects the dross in favour of potential power.

Quimbanda is pro-cosmic. These spirits are all forces that work from the essence of established powers in the world, be it a sentiment, location, shrub or breath. They don't hate, they are full of Saturn, Venus and fire, and if we combine these forces, we always end up with fruits of lasciviousness and wisdom from an old gnarled tree that holds the wisdom of the beginning of times, that seeks outwards in being and effect.

Quimbanda is about tricking the stupid one so he can get smarter as much as it is about standing up for those of power that feel powerless. The realm of Quimbanda is not about exclusion per se, but about recognizing this matrix of power and the knots where it interacts and makes sense and can be of use for us and for them. In other words, we are in the field of 'communion', being a modality that ensures we are always sharp and on the point, and in this our sharpness reflects their edge in our presence.

Exu is there at the cemetery caring for the departed souls as much as he is in the tavern working tricks and enjoying the moment. Pomba Gira can be a stern queen calling our attention as much as she can be a seductive nymph in the woods that challenges you in the name of desire, asking you what you really want.

They are truly spirits of the crossroads everywhere, that moment prior to choice when everything is alive; they made their choices, and teach us of this by calling us back to this crossroad of perpetual choice all the time. In this these sprits become the point and its consequence; a possibility born from choice. And by this quality we recognize the realm of Quimbanda. Exu Sete Estradas making the travel of St. James through the Campostella, finding death in betrayal, and Maria Padilha as the lover of Dom Pedro never reaching the crown of queenship, speak of themes we know, choices we can all make that in the cases of the Exus and Pomba Giras turned into lessons rooted in choices made at the crossroad.

We find that the realm of Quimbanda is composed of any vagabond, any trickster, any knight, any queen or king, any adventurer in whatever kingdom that made that fatal wrong choice, and having done so decided to stay around to ensure that such a choice will never be made again. This is how the Exus understand elevation, I believe—learn from my mistakes and take power from my fire… use the crossroad to your advantage, but in taking advantage you need to realize power wherever it is and in whatever form it shows itself. Saint, sinner, drunkard, king, or yourself—shred it all and see what is truly there and bring it to the crossroad of the nine kingdoms.

Chapter Twelve
The House of Exu

Quem nunca viu venha ver
Who never saw should come and see
caldeirão sem fundo ferver
The bottomless cauldron boiling
quem nunca viu venha ver
Who never saw should come and see
caldeirão sem fundo ferver
The bottomless cauldron boiling
deu meia-noite
It was midnight
cemitério treme
the cemetery rattled
catacumba racha
the catacomb cracked open
e o defunto geme
the dead ones were moaning
deu meia-noite cemitério
it was midnight at the cemetery
treme, catatumba racha
shook the catacomb that cracked open
e o defunto geme
the dead ones were moaning

Preparing sacred space is largely about introducing bonds, limits and attractors to the space you seek to dedicate for the spirits. The terminology used amongst Quimbandeiros to designate the house of Exu varies between *firmeza, tronco, Casa de Exu, tenda, congá, mesa, terreiro, cabula, o reino* and others.

In order to give some idea of the differences and similarities we will discuss, *firmeza, tronco,* and *cabula* will represent the three varieties of dwelling created for Exu that are of a more intimate or domestic level. These suggestions given here are simple ways of structuring the house of Exu, but it is crucial to keep in mind that variations upon these suggestions tend to happen simply because Quimbanda is a living cult that finds its place in each house in ways that are rarely uniform. My intention here is to present an outline that is simple and effective.

The Firmeza

The *firmeza* is the place where you have your statues and items sacred to the cult. It is generally understood to be a place of devotion and representation. There is no demand that the statues be worked or charged, for instance, they can simply be representations that serve as attractors in their own right, and hence a *firmeza* can be understood to be a simple shrine.

Many choose to have their statues on the floor or on the earth, yet others make a table or formal shrine. For the purpose of erecting a *firmeza*, either way is equally good, but something should stay on the ground under the table/shrine. In order to make a proper *firmeza* you will need to get hold of a small *alguidar* (terracotta plate) and wash it in cachaça or vodka. In this vessel you will place one rose quartz and one black onyx (preferably unpolished). You will add to this seven types of peppers, and also earth. At least earth from three crossroads, ocean sand, and river mud should be included in this. If you want to enhance it, add earths from the cemetery (preferably the Cruzeiro) and earths from outside a brothel and/or a cheap tavern. In truth this vessel serves as the attractor of the spirits of Quimbanda, just as preparing your favourite meal would attract you to the table.

This vessel will be placed under the table if you choose to make one, or at the back of the representations of the spirits (preferably in a corner) if you decided to keep them on the ground. A white candle should then be placed in the earth prior to each session and some cachaça or similar added to the earth. It is not necessary to do much more than that in order to work the spirits. You have in doing this set aflame the attractor.

Prior to everything, you will wash the designated place with a fusion of cachaça and lavender, and before placing anything else there, leave three red, three black and one white candle in the place washed to assemble the *firmeza*, placing the vessel in the corner of the place, and let the candles burn out by themselves during the night. The next day you will make your shrine in whatever fashion seems proper, offer cigar fumes to the shrine/*firmeza* and offer some drops of cachaça on the floor.

This will then always be the way you open the *firmeza*:

- A white candle is placed on the vessel that serves as an attractor.
- Red candles (for Pomba Gira) and black candles (for Exu) should be present in a formation of 3 or 7.
- Offerings of alcohol are made and fumes of a cigar and/or cigarillo are blown on the candles and the *firmeza*.
- Draw and sing *pontos*, enter communion and trust the spirit, try to open up and stay with them.

A *firmeza* is not a place where you need to invite in possession, it is a place of veneration. You will at your *firmeza* call upon your personal and working spirits.

The Cabula

To make a proper house for Exu and Pomba Gira is about the presence of *assentamentos*, and a certain spiritual geometry might be involved. In a physical house you will usually find Pomba Gira to the left and the Exus to the right. You will find the enthroned Maioral or Exu Rei elevated above the ground, and everything else is 'on ground', either flat or made in layers like the stairs commonly surrounding the Cruzeiro. When making a house for Exu, a *cabula*, you will observe the colour scheme of red and black.

You will wash the house in champagne and cachaça, and make generous use of lavender and more cachaça, rubbing the house thoroughly in scents and spirits that attract Exu and Pomba Gira.

At the centre of where you will place them you will light coals and feed these coals with pepper, tobacco and drops of cachaça. Even better, make a hole in the ground and do this, and upon this first act you will place the *assentamento* of Omolu—or a similar power. Then you will make something elevated and place the Rei/Maioral there, yet with his *assentamento* on the ground. The Exus go to the right and the Pomba Giras to the left.

You can use tables even in the *cabula*, but then you will still place the *assentamentos* on ground and the statues on the table, because the Exus and Pomba Giras are spirits of earth and it is important to maintain this bond, real or symbolic.

Now, there are of course a multitude of variations on this format, and we do our best with the environment and conditions we have at our disposal. Always keep in mind that Quimbanda is a pragmatic sorcerous cult where we are guided by spirits. We are not doing religion; we are continuing the work and wisdom established by our spirit court.

The Tronco

The term *tronco*, meaning 'stub' or alternatively the trunk of a tree as it shoots from the ground, strictly speaking refers to having the house of Exu seated through a secret process leading to a subterranean assentamento being activated at the door or under the house of Exu. *Tronco* can also refer to a house of Exu that holds *assentamentos*, and the structure and organization of the house is often more intuitive, but also in the *tronco* it can be good to find a place for Exu Omolu as the vessel of attraction for the dead ones, which in some form is placed 'at the bottom' or 'at the back' of the *tronco*. Your personal spirits are placed in the middle and the Maioral of your 'falange'/court is place 'on top' or 'at front'.

A *tronco* is the root of your court and will also be the root of a *cabula*. When a *tronco* is made this hierarchy is somehow replicated, but with proper assentamentos present, and thus we can say that a *tronco* is the true root or foundation of Exu's house.

When a spiritual *tronco* (root/axis) is set up in Quimbanda you will use effigies to represent the spirits. These can be charged or crossed (blessed). You can also use stones, like uncut onyx and obsidian, to represent them. You will then wash the stone in alcohol and raw tobacco and fumigate the stone with rue, peppers and myrrh. You will then place the stone/effigy in a container that holds earth from a crossroad, earth from cemetery, and a pinch of sulfur and peppers. You will draw out the *ponto riscado* and sing the *ponto* as you draw it, and this will then be burnt and placed in the container that holds the stone/effigy.

The place where you want to place the Exu must be washed with alcohol containing rue, pepper and lavender. The *ponto* is marked and the Exu placed over it.

The *tronco* can be a shelf, a cabinet, a house—the point is that it must be a place restricted only to the effigies, where the sunlight is forbidden to enter. It would for instance be fine to arrange the *tronco* in a closed cabinet that is exposed for the sun, but which you can open at night. The idea is that the retinue of Quimbanda quickens as the sun sets, so any work with the *tronco* should be done at sunset (the great hour), during the night, at midnight (the second great hour), or just before daybreak (the third great hour), avoiding letting the rays of the sun hit them.

You will somehow arrange the *tronco* with your personal Exu at the center and his king above him. On a flat surface this will mean that the King is behind your personal Exu; in a cabinet he will be above. It will be beneficial for the *tronco* to get a statue of St. Michael and place him as high as possible to the left of the *tronco*. This St. Michael can be welcomed in the same manner as you do the Exu effigy/stone.

Your personal Exu should be placed at the center, the working Exu at the right and the personal Pomba Gira at the left.

For women and Pomba Gira, red and white roses are added to the alcoholic wash and fumigation, and Pomba Gira takes the center, while the working Exu takes the left.

If Omolu is the King of your Exu, he should take the position of King. If not, he should be placed at the bottom, as the guardian of the chthonic realms; on a flat surface this means that he will be placed in front of the personal Exu. Omolu is always in the equation, so he should be there somewhere.

Thus, the basic *tronco* holds five spirits: your personal Exu, your working Exu, your Pomba Gira, the King/Queen of your personal Exu/Pomba Gira, and Omolu.

The Communion

You will light candles for each of the spirits and offer up cigars and their preferred beverage. You will also give yourself a glass of your preferred beverage and a cigar/cigarillo, and you will sit with them.

You will then sing to them (from the heart):

Pra quimbanda eu vou virar
Towards quimbanda I will turn
Vou chamar todos os Exus
Will call upon all Exus
Para todo mal levar
So They can take away all evil
Oi, dá licença ê
Hi, give me permission, oh!
Oi, dá licença a
Hi, give me permission, oh!
Oi dá licença ê
Hi, give me permission, oh!
Pra fechar nosso congá
to close our shrine

Desci, desci,
Descend, descend
a Quimbanda me chamou
Quimbanda is calling me
Na minha banda sou maior
In my crew I am great
Miguel ainda é maior.
(St.) Michael is even greater

You will then call the King of your Exu using his/her *ponto cantado* and/or this *ponto*:

Oi salve o sol
Oh, greetings Sun
Oi salve a lua /x 3
Oh, greetings Moon /x3
Na encruzilhada
In the Crossroad
Posso com tudo
I can do whatever
Porque eu sou
Because I am
Exu NN
Exu/Pomba Gira NN

You will then call Omolu:

Ê ê, saravá, saravá
Oh, oh, salutations, salutations
O rei Omolú vai chegar
King Omolu is arriving
Ele é o rei
He is the king
Ele é o rei
He is the king

THE HOUSE OF EXU

É o rei da Quimbanda
The King of Quimbanda
É o Maioral
Is the Maioral

You will then call your Exu/Pomba Gira by using the *ponto cantado* and conclude it with:

De certo tem morador /x3
Of course it has a dweller /x3
Na casa que o galo canta
In the house where the rooster sings
Seu Exu é morador
Mr. Exu is the tenant
Na casa que o galo canta
In the house where the rooster sings
De certo tem morador
Of course it has a dweller

At this point you will interact with them and be attentive to words and whispers, energies and impulses. It all forms part of their 'language'. Commune with them, there are no rules here—the objective is to bond with the spirit.

FAREWELL

When the session is over, you will sing the following *pontos* and leave the *tronco*, allowing the candles to burn down by themselves.

Vai embora Exu
Take your leave Exu
Não tropeça no caminho
Do not stumble on the path
Passa no quintal dos outros

Walk through the Garden of eveyone
Mas não mexa com vizinho
But don't mess with the neighbours

Miguel mandou, te coroou
Miguel sent you, crowned you
Fogo de palha pra Exu
Fire in the hay for Exu
Ir embora
Take your leave
Miz Angola
My Angola
Auê, caminho de Angola
Ah, the road of Angola
Que Exu vai embora
Is where Exu takes his leave

Chapter Thirteen
Working Macumba

Sou exu, trabalho no canto
I am Exu, and I work in the song
Quando canto desmancho quebranto
When the song breaks the broken pieces
Sete cordas tem minha viola
Seven strings on my violin
Vou na gira de lenço e cartola
I go to the gira with scarf and tophat
Viola é tridente
The Violin is the Trident
Cigarro é charuto
Cigarette is the Cigar
Bebida é marafo
The drink is cachaça
Sou Sete da Lira
I am Mr. Seven of the Lyre
Derrubo inimigo
Knocking down the enemy
Ponteiro de aço
Pointer of Steel

Working magic in the context of Quimbanda is frequently called 'to do macumba', and macumba is done with the assistance of spirit; as the *ponto cantado* goes, 'without Exu we can't do anything'. Before discussing various forms of *macumba*, also known as *magia negra* or 'black magic', it is important to understand the spiritual technology behind working *macumba*. Since Quimbanda always entails the involvement of a spirit that is central to the execution of the work, there are some considerations worthy to take into account.

Given the amoral orientation of Exu and how this power has a mercurial ability to reflect the summoner, the approach we take in involving Exu is important to consider. Earlier in this book the ideas of helping Exu to evolve into a benign spirit by the assistance of more evolved spiritual beings and thus training Exu to be educated and upright was mentioned. These thoughts are not without their merits, but have perhaps been presented in a biased way, assuming Exu is by essential nature dark, demonic and dangerous. It is more correct to say that he is also this, and like all spirits nocturnal and chthonic, some rapport with the dangerous and hidden is naturally present. The issue is more that Exu, in theory, will agree to whatever contract is offered as long as the word is the bond and the payment is given. Hence, if you approach Exu as a hitman or fixer, this is the relationship you will establish, and just as in the human world, the fixer hired to do a job doesn't care what happens with you as long as you pay what was agreed.

Given that blood, tobacco, spirits, and fire are food and corporal mist for these amoral spirits, it is theoretically possible to make a *quid pro quo* deal with Exu and Pomba Gira concerning anything. Now, taking that same fixer and discovering that you have an affinity for one another, and you start cultivating these affinities and establishing a bond of friendliness and respect, this will invite into the workings a very different quality of the fixer. If we add to this that the fixer is the spirit of a dead one that makes up part of a legion of similar but distinct spirits where he has access to both his own knowledge from life and the collective wisdom of his legion to impart and teach, it might be better to choose the course that takes time, where Exu is approached as a spirit guide, as a Tata of the woods in league with mystery and wisdom beyond our perception. In extension of this it is also important to understand the difference between the quick fix and the long game of fixing life. Exu is extremely helpful in both scenarios, but a quick fix is rarely long-lasting, whilst bringing Exu into our life in a committed way, as a guide in life, makes us agile, perceptive and always ready to engage with life, the world, and the situations rising from the many crossroads we encounter in our journey on earth.

On this basis, working macumba can be as simple as offering a bottle of cachaça and a cigar to have something done, up to multiple life force offerings to achieve the same results. It depends on several factors, one of them being what type of relationship we have with Exu and on what premises he agreed to work. In addition to this it is also about how realistic the goals set for the macumba are. Let us remember that magic, spell work or macumba in the Middle Ages was a serious discipline under the heading of natural philosophy; it was about understanding the hidden or occult workings of nature. These occult secrets consisted in understanding how doing something in one place could generate effects in another place, namely by understanding the vinculum between all things in the worlds, visible and invisible, and how all things were connected. Understanding this would lead to the knowledge of manipulating these bonds, hence practical magic, or macumba. The first modality is how we fuel the occult engine of Exu to effectuate something in the material world, which we do through offerings, of which the most common one is the *padê*.

A *padê* is basically a *farofa*, or in some cases a polenta, that is served in a dish. It is made from manioc or corn flour stirred in with palm oil and hot pepper sauce. The *padê* can be made over the fire or not. From this basic dish of flour with palm oil and pepper sauce, myriad variations can be found depending on what is sought to be accomplished through the offering. For instance, from this basic dish, if we add raw beef and vinegar we have a *padê* that is pleasing for the people of the Cemetery, like Exu Caveira, Tata Caveira and João Caveira. If we add to the mixture honey we are pulling in the qualities of Pomba Gira, and if seven thornless roses are offered on top of this we have a simple but functional *agrado*, meaning a gift with the intent of pleasing a spirit, for Pomba Gira. To the *padê* can be added coins or money cowry to bring in the wish for prosperity and gain, as much as the offerings of pomegranates and apples along with the *agrado* for Pomba Gira will signal an erotic element. The dish in which the *padê* is served can very well be prepared by drawing the *ponto riscado* of the Exu in question with *pemba*[17] in the bottom. As the food is prepared, *pontos* are sung, just as they are also sung when offering in front of the spirit.

When the *padê* is brought to the *firmeza* it is flanked by candles, and proper alcoholic beverages and tobacco are offered both in front of the effigies and to the *padê*. In addition to these fundamental items, popcorn, meat, roses, perfumes, natural objects of a great variety, and life force offerings can make up part of the offering depending on what the goal might be and what Exus and Pomba Giras are being worked. At this point petitions can be given and communion should take place. Hence, a simple setting like this will raise sufficient energy to be directed towards a desired goal and achieve results.

When making food for spirits we are investing the energy of the host into what we are preparing, to welcome our guests. We are using elements that hold a reference, preference and resonance with the powers we want to summon, both in terms of virtue pure and simple, and in terms of the virtue of memory, both of people and of culture.

In the case of the *padê*, this food came from Africa and fast became a staple food in Brazil, hence the *padê* or *farofa* does represent the memory of Africa as much as the continuation of this memory in Brazil. To this basic food of memory, culture and preference we add what is of the virtue of the spirit, namely peppers and palm oil, the latter representing blood and nutrition, the former representing the quality of the spirits we are working with. The onions added to the *padê* are not only fiery and watery at the same time, but are also a tool for divination, hence we invite the spirit to speak and open communication in introducing onion rings. The coins or cowry shells represent money, but also increase, and are ultimately a symbol of trade, that we are giving something and expect something back. The peppers usually placed in the *padê* will then both represent our exaltation of the spirits we are feeding and summoning, as well as enhance the bond between

---

17 Chalk.

what is offered and what is summoned by the pure representation of what is red, hot and fiery. In essence, by feeding spirits in this way we invite in their presence in a similar manner as we do when we prepare food for a guest in ways we know will be to their liking, and with the arrival of the guest is when the magic happens.

The singing of *pontos* and offering up of alcohol and tobacco enables Exu and Pomba Gira to take shape and become present. Through this food for the spirit, through the fires of peppers, alcohol and tobacco, the Exus and Pomba Giras are able to become present and tangible in this moment of communion.

It is important to realize that everything done in Quimbanda is meaningful, and the more we understand the meaning and symbolism beneath the elements of cult we use, the more efficiently we will enter into the bond of communion and be subject to receiving our guest, be it by inspiration, possession, automatic writing and drawing, or whatever is a natural skill on the part of the medium summoning them.

All efficient *macumba* is based on this form of care and understanding of why we are doing what we are doing. Quimbanda is rooted in connection with spirits and so it is crucial to develop this bond in truth and earnest acceptance.

When spirits speak, they can do so by images, whispers, impressions and sensations, as much by a 'voice in the head' and direct possession as by automatic writing. The bridge for communication is less important than the honesty about what is going on and the acceptance of what is the natural connection, as well as refraining from deception, including of oneself. This is important because we are dealing with real spirits, an invisible reality with the power to influence our reality. The *farofa*, palm oil, peppers, tobacco, blood and alcohol are mediums through which we fuel and set on fire and give shape to these spirits so they can affect the material world; we are offering up virtues that enable them to take shape.

And there we are at the heart of *macumba*: it is something that happens in this field where the invisible meets the material and has some form of consequence related to our aim and direction.

It is important to address the nature of pacts at this point. People tend to make a great deal of the existence of pacts, and naturally a pact is a great deal, but at the end of the day it is about commitment, word and concord, so if this comes easy for you to uphold, a pact should not be problematic to observe. The problem is that humankind usually break their pacts, as they break their word, loyalty and contracts between one another, due to whatever selfish explanation and reasoning they use to justify such lack of honour. It is from this that we have the many tales speaking of how pacts with spirits turn into demonic alliances that send the pact maker into a rut and madness. A pact is simply an agreement, a treaty, to fix, fasten or bring something into a union of concord and mutual aid. It is not a bad thing, but if one party starts to delay and defile their part of the treaty, then problems usually occur, whether it is a contract of marriage or a treaty between politicians or businessmen. The treaty most often broken is the treaty of confidence between friends and married couples, and of course people who break bonds easily amongst one another also tend to do this with even greater frequency with invisible counterparts.

If we understand this simple premise to be at the root of pact making, if we understand preparing a meal of calculated virtue to be about honouring what we invite in with commitment and honour, we will not have much problem in obtaining results. Lack of results often tends to be relegated to explanations rooted in our own lack of understanding and lack of compromise, replicating our inherent casual nonchalant attitude towards pacts in general. As above, so below, and so it is at all eight corners of the crossroad…

Three elements rarely discussed when it comes to practical magic and spell work are placebo magic, chimerical magic, and nefarious magic, but when it comes to Quimbanda these concepts are of great importance. Let us start with the latter, nefarious magic, which basically rests on the question, 'even if you can do it, should you do it?' 'Nefarious' does speak of something villainous and unethical; the moral dimension enters into play, not strictly in relation to divine law, but more in the sense of what goes around comes around. It is about what occult, magical and energetic circuits we perpetuate and stimulate to affect the world, as it also includes our involvement in the process and the results. The most obvious example of nefarious magic is perhaps workings to attract death, loss and illness, but it is also possible to argue that love bindings are nefarious, in the sense that the will, desire, happiness and attraction of a person are thwarted towards a less than benign goal.

The moral dimensions aside, the thwarting and breaking of natural bonds is a serious issue, and it is perhaps wise to contemplate this dimension prior to planning a working of this calibre. One story can exemplify how this nefarious way can lead to grim results. In this story a man came to a Quimbandeiro asking for help. He wanted his wife back. After all, they had children and he had turned away from his violent and drunken ways. The Quimbandeiro turned him away, but he came back, desperate and drunk. The Quimbandeiro told him that if he managed to stay sober for a week the binding could be done. He stayed sober for a week and the binding was done. Three days later he came back furious: the binding didn't work, it was all worse now than before! How can it be worse now than before? the Quimbandeiro asked, and the man said that his estranged wife had finally answered his call and had after months of not wanting to see him agreed to see him. He went there expecting it all to be perfect, but she just wanted to talk and refused his sexual advances, so he did what any violent drunkard would do in a situation like that, he beat her up, leading to a police report and divorce instead of the union he was searching for.

In this terrible situation it was a Queen Pomba Gira that agreed to do the love binding, just to show that this was not the way to go, and ultimately the woman got free from the abusive man through this last violence and found happiness with another man, whilst her ex-husband withered away, perpetually drunk, depressed and forgotten in a shed in the middle of nowhere. In other words, even if you can do it, should you do it? Was the violence sort of 'justified' because the end was good, or was it just the wrong call on behalf of the Quimbandeiro? There is no easy answer to those questions, but the answer is of no importance, the contemplation of the matter is.

Placebo magic is magic that is done by someone who doesn't really have any connection with their spirit guide. Theatrics are performed and some amount of energy is generated by the sacrificial items and the will power, the rest is generated by belief. Belief is truly a marvellous force, and it lies beneath the form of faith that brings forth miracles, but there is also the placebo magic that consists in looking for alternative signs and realizations that would affirm something supernatural at play, whilst what is at play is only the natural and marvellous powers of faith. The use of faith for generating results, be it a placebo or genuine magic, is not unlike how charismatic movements generate high level emotional vibrations and then project will and determination towards a given goal.

Chimeric magic wants to bind sentiments, emotions and feelings into a state, situation or subject, with disregard of bonds. It is a magic fuelled by desire and will alone, that does not hold as requisite that the person doing what he or she is doing truly has a pact with a spirit for results to become evident and tangible. This is very different from projecting a wish or desire into the world in the presence of a spirit, as is often the case with spirit workers, who don't question their own character, nature or reason for the working unless it is about some good money offered to bring back what was lost or gain what is desired.

Effective macumba, however, is born from one's spiritual capacity and intensity of bond with one's spirit guide. It is about the understanding of bonds and virtues. It is about understanding why we do what we do, and it is about realizing that the invisible and the material exist in a shared reality and getting to grips with how this dynamic works to our favour and disfavour. Our model is an interaction between ourselves and some influential guest, and the pact, accord and treaty comes from this meeting. In other words, macumba is rooted in the intensity of the liaison we have with a spirit, not our desire, fire, anger or will, but the connection. It is in this bond and the understanding of it that we execute wisdom and make macumba.

Chapter Fourteen
To Bind Desire

Vinha caminhando a pé
I came travelling on foot
para ver se encontrava a
to see if I could meet
minha cigana de fé
My gypsy of faith
Vinha caminhando a pé
I came travelling on foot
para ver se encontrava a
to see if I could meet
minha cigana de fé
My gypsy of faith
Parou e leu minha mão
Stopped to read my hand
Me disse a pura verdade
Told me all what was true
E eu só queria saber
I only wanted to know
onde mora Pomba Gira Cigana
Where Pomba Gira Gyspy lives
só queria saber
I only wanted to know
onde mora Pomba Gira Cigana.
Where Pomba Gira Gypsy lives

Workings aiming towards binding 'love', affection, sexual interest and lust are, together with workings for harming others and receiving wealth and riches, the most sought-after workings. After this comes requests for forms of healing, reparation, and good fortune.

A love binding is in truth rarely about love; more commonly it is about binding desire and lust, exercised by one subject and transferred upon an object of desire. Arguably love, passions, fascinations and attractions are all instigated by the presence of eros, the very same eros that Plato understood to be a divine quicksilver that through contemplation can be made to remember the true cosmic beauty, but when rushed instead attaches with passion to material and terrestrial beauty. Eros can be understood as a fire by its capacity for setting emotions and passions aflame, and also the quicksilver/mercury quality would make eros a force subjectable and workable by Exu, and especially by Pomba Gira who is so akin to eros through her voluptuous, fascinating, and concupiscent presence.

A working done to bind a couple consists in appealing to Pomba Gira on behalf of women and to Exu on behalf of men, and the work of binding takes the form of simple poppet spells accompanied by a proper *padê*.

Let us take the example of a woman wanting a man. A *padê* of corn flour mixed with palm oil, peppers and honey is made as a base. In this we find elements representing blood (palm oil), fire (peppers) and sweetness (honey), which serve as good rustic bonds to attract desire to what is presented, and hence we have in the presentation of the *padê* already the energetic bond we seek to cause the desired effect. To this *padê* is then added cloves and cinnamon sticks, cowry shells, and fruits that hold the virtue of passion, like apples, pomegranates, peaches, and such.

The names of the couples are written crossed on seven pieces of paper, and some are pierced by the cloves while others are placed inside the fruits by cutting them in half, naming each of the parts, and tying them back together with cords of black, red and white, then placing the fruit in the centre of the *padê*. Pomba Gira is called to witness the working and to perform the work asked for, and the blood of a proper animal, champagne, cigarillos and perfume are added to the offering as the aim is repeatedly stated in between the *pontos* that are constantly sung.

It is also possible to introduce dolls, that are 'baptized' or named by sprinkling them with cachaça and/or holy water with the names of the two people placed inside the respective dolls, which are then tied together with threads of black, red and white, drenched in honey and then placed on the *padê*.

It is customary to declare a payment of three times what was offered to ensure that Pomba Gira will do the work successfully—and when success is claimed it is important to execute the promise within seven days as a thanksgiving and insurance that the bond continues to be active.

Now, all this is fine in structure; we call a spirit known to have a clear effect on matters of the heart, lust, and desire, and we are presenting a deal for the spirit, a pact if you wish. If the Quimbandeiro doing this work has a true and good connection with the spirit, a working like this usually works, but this is not always the case, even when the Quimbandeiro has such a connection with the spirit.

When a working like this fails, it is due to one of three things that are worthy of a deeper assessment:
- There is no bond between the two people to work.
- The situation was not properly analysed.
- The client lied about the situation at hand.

In assessing the issues that might block the desired result we are returning to the importance of understanding what is going on in a situation so we can introduce the correct bonds for a spirit to work with. In a way, assessing the tools of spiritual work is like any other situation related to building something. If we want to make a stove, we need to apply bricks and cement to the design and use the proper tools for accomplishing the goal. In short, to continue the example given, if this woman is seeking to be reunited with her husband or boyfriend, we need to think differently about how we execute the work than in a case where a woman wants someone she has no prior bond with, just a fascination. In the case of the first situation, to be reunited or to see a union take shape between two people who actually have a mutual affinity towards one another, the work detailed will usually be sufficient.

Yet, if we are speaking of a situation between two people who have gone awry, and let us say the man she seeks to have back has already moved on and is no longer feeling 'attached' to her, we are confronted with a completely different situation as we need to completely remake a bond between the two, and thus a work like that detailed here which aims towards making sweet a bond that is already present will usually not work.

In a case like this we need to get creative and analytic, we need to ask the spirit to give us counsel in dreams or visions and we need to contemplate how we can manipulate matter in order to generate a field of resonance between the two subjects.

In forcing a bond, possessing organic items from both persons, like hair, nails, skin, underwear, or cloth containing sweat, saliva, blood or sexual fluids, will be the way to go, and these can then be tied together in the presence of the spirit and offered to the spirit as a link and thread to follow.

In cases of a more illusory nature, when someone asks to bond with a celebrity for instance, we are speaking of something else than a binding, we are speaking of desires bound in dreams, and that is a whole different ballgame—in theory possible, but to manifest dreams in the vinculum of desire between two people who have no sub-lunar mutual bond is truly a task better left alone, due to the time and patience it demands to work these bonds step by step.

More simple strategies tend to be just as effective, and of these we can mention a few that we find in the arsenal of folk magic and sorcery in various parts of the world and also in Brazil.

One of these is to take your used underwear and use this as a filter for making coffee or tea to serve to the one of whose desire you seek to be the object. Naturally this can be used to filter wine and water as well, the idea being that the virtue of your genitals constitutes part of what is consumed by the one whom you wish to feel desire for you.

Another strategy is to add vaginal fluids, semen, menstrual blood or a drop of blood from the Venus Mount on your left hand to some beverage and serve it to the object of desire.

Yet another strategy is for a woman to masturbate herself until climax with, for instance, a cucumber, keeping the object of desire in mind, and then serve this vegetable to be eaten by the object of desire.

All these strategies are bond-making in essence. It will work like throwing out an anchor from a boat: the anchor fastens in the ground and establishes a bond from ocean floor to boat through the chain of the anchor—and workings like this aim towards establishing that form of resonance.

This will give you some idea of the types of bonds that can be used in a binding spell and how to obtain them.

In relation to such workings we need to be clear that we are not binding love, but rather desire, hence we will work with our sorcerous arsenal in relation to this fact, and so herbs like damiana, mandrake, and nightshades in general are examples of the virtues we can introduce that are tied to desire and ecstasy and also to the property of transgressing the conscious mind and working what is beneath what we restrict. This is because most people are not driven by love when they ask for a binding work, but by desire. Desire is the child of Venus, but it is not love, rather it is a force that serves as an amalgam between things, as a Mercury drenched in the honey and herbs of lust.

Because of this it is so crucial to analyse any situation that asks for a bond, to see what is truly at play. A bond between an abusive man and a submissive woman who wants to get away from the abuser is very different from the bonds and virtues at play between a couple who have been estranged from one another yet one still seeks the other and the one she or he seeks is still harbouring desires for the seeker as well.

In this field we need to exercise discernment and cunning, and in all this we are also adding our own energy as a bonding agent with spirit that stretches out to the couples. Quite simply we give what we have and we have success in working what we have; a person who has no love in his or her life will not be successful in working bonds of love, whilst a person full of desire that gets laid whenever he or she wants will have success in bindings due to the simple mechanisms of natural bonds and vivid virtues present within the practitioner.

In conclusion, the bonds and virtues of a binding are rooted in shared symmetry, like the apple cut in half, names placed in between and tied together, in sweetness (like honey), in things that agitate, like peppers, and of course the cord must always be present, and even better if it is a knotted cord. The knotted cord involves making knots on a leather cord, with the names of the couple inside each knot sealed with breath, intent, honey and peppers to bind the two subjects together in a ladder of desire.

The field of binding eros and desire provides a rich treasure-trove of possibilities, and in this we should also consider the binding in general. It doesn't need to be between two subjects; it is possible to use the same technology to bind yourself to something else, like a work, a place, or what you wish, by working this bond of desire in clever and cunning ways.

Chapter Fifteen
Murderous Sorcery

Maria Padilha é uma feiticeira
Maria Padilha is a sorceress
mas não gosta de falar
but she doesn't like to talk
Maria Padilha é um a feiticeira
Maria Padilha is a sorceress
mas não gosta de falar
but she doesn't like to talk
O feitiço que ela faz
The magic she does
ela faz é pra matar
She does to kill
O feitiço que ela faz
The magic she does
ela faz é pra matar
She does to kill

✦✦✦✦✦✦✦✦✦✦✦✦

Tentaram me matar com
They tried to kill me with
um copo de veneno
a cup of poison
Tentaram me matar com
They tried to kill me with
um copo de veneno
a cup of poison
Quem quiser matar me mate
Who wants to kill me, just kill me
Que beber eu bebo mesmo ...
Wanting me to drink, I will drink it…

Workings that seek to murder and annihilate someone are amongst the most difficult workings to actually make result in the demise of the target, because these types of workings are bound by a host of vinculums and connections that need to be unravelled and worked.

In the realm of murderous sorcery we can count workings that aim towards the removal of someone's spiritual protection, as this factor is quite integral to the working's success. This is perhaps why one of the most dangerous workings in this realm is to perform the Requiem, or the Mass of the Dead, for a living person nine Saturdays in a row. This is because the Mass is indistinctly focused on the soul of the deceased, hence saying a Mass for the departed for a living person will invite in a very different sort of attention from the powers of the other side in overseeing the departure of the soul they have been asked to take notice of. Naturally the Mass should be recited by an ordained cleric in order to have ultimate power, which is why the rituals that break or sever the contact with a person's guardian angel are more frequently used, a procedure that often decides success or failure in operations of this quality.

There are many ways of doing this, but if the bond with Exu is strong, a white candle can be lit in the honour of the target. This candle is inscribed with the name of the target and anointed with oil. Midway in the candle two razorblades are inserted in such a way that when the flame reaches the blades it is extinguished. The murderous working then is commenced after the fire of the guardian spirit is extinguished on the blades, giving a certain window of time for the *maleficium* to do its work with less interference from protective spirits. Another variant of this ritual is to use seven white candles, inscribe them all with the name of the person, anoint them with oil and prepare a simple offering of meat and red wine and water for the guardian angel on a white cloth. These seven candles are placed in a circle around the offering and at a certain point the seven candles are broken, extinguished and left in the dish. This will then give some time to work *maleficia*, and if one seeks to agitate the target in the absence of their protection, pepper sauce and a piece of anthill with living ants is added to the disastrous meal.

The effects of murderous sorcery can play out in very different ways, but the usual trajectory is the onset of a series of misfortunes accompanied by the slow growth of illness whose cause manages to occult itself during medical investigation. A hostile atmosphere is generated that grows and expands, making the target susceptible to demise in various accidental ways. For instance, the working involving the heart of a bull or similar, in which the target is literally—and through the intercession of a spirit, also magically—stabbed to death by the use of large nails, knives, or daggers, usually marks the beginning of affliction. Yet a working like this can also see the death of the target in the very same night as the working is done. The effectiveness of the working depends on several factors, and the first of these involves the bond the target has with the Fates, the energetic situation of the target, the medical situation of the target, and the target's temperament. In addition to this, the bond the spirit worker has with the target is also important, and it appears that quite often the French saying that 'revenge is a dish best served cold' is also true for murderous sorcery. Somehow it seems that workings of this calibre are better fuelled by cold reason and a focused yet nonchalant attitude than by hatred and anger.

In considering the target and the effectiveness of a malefic working, consider first the standing of the target with the Fates. The Fates, or Moirai, were the spirits that gave each man and woman their lot in life, and in this also the length of years. We find Clotho who spun the thread of life, Lachesis that decided its length and quality, and Atropos, 'the un-turnable', who cut this thread. This means that if an immediate result of one's murderous sorcery was achieved, the target had it coming. The working was something that the target was attracting to themselves at this very juncture as the means of severing the cord of life. In antiquity, the only force that could actually meddle with a person's destiny was Nemesis, the spirit of retribution, with her scales, measuring rod and sword. It is common to think about her as some sort of opposing force, but in truth the only force she is opposing is Lady Fortuna, hence she is tangible to us as the presence of misfortune. In antiquity, the way of calling Nemesis down upon your life was to display hubris and bad character overall, but she could also be called upon as an intercessor, as someone you would appeal to on the premise that she would take a good look at a given person who had fallen prey to the terrible vice of hubris, which would bar fortune from the person's life as Nemesis's attention was upon them. This factor in play could then cause an accident or early demise to occur along the thread of that person's life.

The target's energetic situation, health and temperament are also important factors to take into consideration. For instance, renowned politicians are subject to magical attacks and murderous sorcery quite often, but with quite poor results. This is partly due to the absence of correct knowledge amongst spirit workers, as much as incorrect assessment of the energetic nature of the target. Let's continue with the example of a politician of some notoriety. When a magical attack is directed towards this person, the first error is made. This is because a politician is not a normal person, they are a face given to a hybrid composed of an ideology, a political party and political ambition within a greater energetic political cluster that provides energetic dead ends and potential confusion along the occult pathway by which the magic aims to do its work. It is like attacking a maze and not a man, and such considerations are important when we assess what elements need to be present in the working.

The consequences of a high energetic protection and being subject to attention from various corners and places simultaneously generates a complex network, if not a wall, that causes sorcerous acts aiming towards the end of the target to work only in partial ways because there are simply too many energetic factors involved; it might end up being like arrows hitting a concrete wall, which is the case with people in power who are aided in strange ways by those who flock around them to provide this energetic protection. Yet another factor of importance is to measure well the character of the target. For instance, a person that is choleric and places themself in compromising situations of conflict and potential danger will be a far easier target than someone of a more stoic nature. A person that demonstrates self-control, endurance and a desire towards general betterment is a difficult target to take down, as doing this will in general require a high number of repetitions of the working because the magical attack will be like chiselling away on a stone, piece by piece. Repetition of workings is also something to take into account, as repeating the same work over an extended period of time, always on the same day and hour, will rapidly increase the magical punch.

Lastly, in terms of the stature of the target, we also have the power and protection that come through initiations or the bonds made by binding oneself to spirits and cosmic forces that naturally bring various levels of protection against the effects of *maleficia*, and metaphorically change a person's spiritual signature. In short, a person of good character, possessing virtues like self-control and endurance, who has undergone several forms of initiations into traditional cults, will be an amazingly difficult target. In the same vein, when there is some scuffle between *macumbeiros* that leads to magical attacks, it is important to consider the fact that when you send your Exu to deal with your adversary, this Exu might find himself quite at home with the proposed target and hence the attack doesn't end in much beyond the scuffle and irritation on a merely debased human level. Of course, it is possible for such attacks to work due to some friction between the Exus, most often involving other spirit guides or 'imposter Exus', what we call *kiumbas* or larvae.

The observation of these elements is crucial for assessing the effect that can be expected from a given work, but let us have a look at the classical doll-and-coffin workings from a Quimbanda perceptive.

Basically, you will fashion a poppet from cloth, corn husks or beeswax. You will baptize the effigy in the name of the target with water to which you have added a pinch of salt, and you will take a number of pins that are washed in pepper, sulphur and vinegar and affix them to vital points on the effigy corresponding to the parts of the target's body you seek to harm, such as head, heart, lungs or liver. The effigy is then veiled in black cloth and placed in a coffin. The coffin is filled with cemetery dirt, sulphur, vinegar and asafoetida. Some also add faeces of cat and dog to the contents of the coffin. This coffin is then brought to the cemetery where it is buried as close to the Cruzeiro as possible, offering a candle and some tobacco and cachaça to Exu Omolu as payment for use, and also to garner his attention. Alternatively, the coffin is placed in a fresh grave or a newly opened grave, and thus placed in the earth beneath the dead one that is to be buried there. You will light a single white candle and declare the death of the one you seek to murder, and if possible, a stone or cross is also erected in memory of the one you seek to harm. You will stay there violently visualizing his or her death, and at the end you will break the candle and throw it in or on the grave, take three steps back, turn around and leave without looking back.

A working like this is naturally done at night, and it is important to use the left hand as much as possible.

All such workings are done under the auspices of some power, and they can be done with the aid of Exu Caveira, Exu Tatá Caveira, Exu Sete Cruzes, Exu Sete Lombas, Exu Nove Luzes, Exu Morcego and many others. In the end what is of more importance is the connection you have with the Exu in question, and to some, albeit secondary, extent, what would be the natural bent or speciality of the Exu in question.

In order to enhance the effects of the ritual, it can be repeated by returning to the grave for nine consecutive Mondays and performing a Requiem Mass or similar over the grave; alternatively it can be done for nine nights in a row. The grave is given one white candle that is broken at the conclusion and left at the grave, and the grave is fed with vinegar and chrysanthemum.

When we look at this classic working, we see that we are using either Monday or Sunday due to the virtue these days hold. Sunday is a day of rest, but it is also when the Church is active, and hence the sorcerer can freely make heretical use of this potency being active on that day to seek his own goals.

Mondays are preferred due to the Moon being cyclical and going through a monthly death—hence when the Moon is waning into her quarter of blackness is naturally the phase we want to elect for such work. Another auspicious moment is when a funeral is actually being performed and we have the opportunity to perform our funeral at the same time. Lastly Eastertide, when the death of Jesus happened, is also a good time, as is the winter solstice, being the day with the longest night. Naturally, other options would be Tuesday, ruled by Mars, and Saturday, ruled by Saturn, depending on whether a violent death or an early putrid grave is sought.

Looking at the ritual itself we find that it is a work of sympathy and replication, a transference of virtues from a person unto an effigy or object, and we should note that in ancient Mesopotamia similar rituals were done with the purpose of causing death, but also in works of transferring illness from a person to an object or an animal that was then subjected to a funeral in place of the ill person. Hence in workings like this we work a sorcery of transference, and knowing this we will also know how to bind the working properly between representation and goal.

We have also other methods of seeking the death of a person. Again we need a representation of the person; a poppet, a piece of cloth, nails, hair, a photo can all be used, but of course vary in strength as a bond maker. These magnetic items are then tied with a cord—if it is possible to obtain thread or cloth from a corpse, even better—and the contents soaked in unpleasant and lethal ingredients that should hold some harmony with the virtue of the person we seek to harm as well as the harm we seek. This means, if the target likes strawberries and bacon, we might add these to the personal items along with mercury, nails and *arrebenta cavalo* (*Solanum platanifolium*), sealing the vessel and throwing it away in the ocean, in a well, in the garbage or from a cliff, or simply leave it in a ditch at the highway.

The place we choose is important for the way we seek the death of the target, and also here we will benefit from knowing the target's habits and behaviours. Such a 'vessel of death' placed

MURDEROUS SORCERY

in a ditch at the highway for someone who is known to drive like a madman will link the target and the use of vehicles on the highway, and because a bond of that nature was already in place, it will be fortified.

These workings are quite generic and we find variations of them in all corners of the world, not only in Quimbanda, but as we see, the sorcerous technology is again about generating bonds and tying them together in occult and sorcerous ways to enable our goal.

All workings done at the feet of our Exu will have a greater effect than rituals done in the absence of a particular spirit, as they would then attract whatever loose, wandering and hungry soul was roaming around to do the work.

Payment for the work is also important. In the case of the work being rooted in a pact with Exu, we will offer blood, *padê* and generous amounts of cachaça and tobacco to Exu, which will serve as thanksgiving and also 'fuel'—which means that we should also consider offering *padê* and blood when the work is requested, as it will serve as fuel for the spirit to push the work through.

In the cases where we are simply working with *kiumbas* found at the cemetery under the watchful eyes of Exu Omolu, upon the work's success we will offer up something to Exu Omolu, like seven white and three black candles along with some tobacco, some red wine and whiskey, and we will also feed the grave with red wine, tobacco, and two coins.

Yet, as stated, workings like this are not easy, it all depends on the 'fate of a man' how successful a working like this will be. Yet some effect is often attained, be it in terms of difficulties in the target's life, accidents, illness, loss of grace or misfortunes in general.

It is also worthy to consider that workings of such calibre might hold some heavy luggage, as we are here taking the position of judge of the living and the dead, a position that in the material world implies a given set of skills, a certain objectivity and adherence to facts that might be difficult to achieve in a situation where a magical attack is at play. It is also important to keep in mind that when we play with gunpowder and fire there is always a risk involved in how they will behave, and also whether or not we get scolded in the process. Lastly, if we do prepare the demise of a person, it is virtually impossible to not get contaminated on some level; thinking we can deal with poisons, toxic ashes and dense earth without getting a smudge here and there is not really realistic.

During workings like this it is paramount to keep one's spirit high, work benevolence, give alms, do favours to counter the working's contagion, and make daily baths of sea salt and rue to avoid *larvae* and ghostly presences becoming attached to you.

Chapter Sixteen
Works of Gain and Money

Vem, vem pro terreiro
Come come to the temple
vem pra trabalhar
Come to work
vem, vem pro terreiro
Come come to the temple
saravando Exu Chama-Dinheiro
Saluting Exu that brings money
de onde vem esse exu
from where this Exu comes
no seu cruzeiro só tem riqueza
at his point of power there is only wealth
ele trabalha na linha das almas
he works in the line of the souls
ajudando o povo com sua clareza
helping people with his clairvoyance

In Quimbanda we find a rich arsenal of workings for money and gain, the most famous one being the *patuá* built upon the 'lucky dime', which can be obtained from some cheap tavern, the coins given as return for having luck in gambling, or a coin taken or given from a beggar or a *malandro*. The word patuá is a Tupi word meaning 'sachet', but is today a word meaning amulet, similar to a mojo hand.

We see in this the presence of a form of contagious magic, where somehow a volt of monetary gain is encoded into the object as if it were a talisman in its own right (which it actually is).

Such items naturally invite working their bonds by different avenues. The coin obtained from a beggar will be worked in a different way than the coin obtained from a *malandro*, as in the case of the latter we will work bonds of opportunity while in the former we will work in a more mysterious field of increase in all senses.

As always when working a patuá of good fortune based on some talismanic prophylactic item, such as a coin in this example, we need to consider both the situation and the person from which it was obtained. And in this I really want to invite in some creative juggling of the bonds present, because there should really be no hard and fast rule in this, yet, to give an example:

You are sitting at a tavern and a beggar comes along and you give some coins (which you in most cases should do, as generosity towards those who have nothing replicates a bond of nearly cosmic generosity in favour of both the giver and the receiver) and then he drops one of the coins. That is a golden moment; take the coin and if necessary buy it from the beggar by offering more than what was dropped, but keep the coin. You will then present this coin to the Mulambos in the *tronco*, and you will add to this coin mustard and sesame seeds, which are traditional symbols of the increase of what is presented, in this case, coin/money. You will add some dirt from outside a bank or from houses in a wealthy neighbourhood, along with seven peppers and something from the ocean. You will then gather it all in either raffia cloth or a rag and sew it together with red and white threads. You will then feed it by calling Pomba Gira Mulambo or Exu Ganga and feeding it candles, red wine, cachaça, cigar—and in this case you will also add incense of a Lunar or Jupiterian quality.

This patuá will then serve as an attractor, given the particular bond we are working here, which will be one of opportunity and the fortification of luck.

A similar patuá can be made with the aid of Zé Pelintra or any Exu or Pomba Gira living in the kingdom of the Ocean Shore or the Lyre, where the coin, obtained from a *malandro*, prostitute or rich person, holds the same value—it is all about the money and the gain—hence you will in this case add some jurema root or bark along with herbs that hold a virtue of money, gain and increase, like fern, roses, rosemary and many, many others. You will present this to Zé Pelintra and offer him cognac with lemon

WORKS FOR GAIN AND MONEY

and honey, a cigar and candles, red, white and black, leave it overnight and then wrap it up in velvet or linen. This form of patuá is said to be good for gambling and also to be worn when you want to negotiate deals or are applying for work.

As we see, all these workings, from the simple concept of a patuá, hold hard and fast in their hand the concept of chance and luck, and so we need to place ourselves out in the world for the patuá to be effective. We need to allow ourselves to move in the world and in this way we give further force to this moveable energy we know as money.

The same concept is present in all forms of workings aiming towards gain and money; for instance if we want to make a *padê* to obtain money, in order to fuel the spirit correctly the *padê* cannot be hard or dry, it must be wet and soft, and items from the ocean (natural significator of wealth) along with dust of gold and silver must be added to the offering as well as good, expensive meat, good expensive drinks and so forth. Of herbs, cinnamon and nutmeg make part of it, along with honey and seven types of peppers that give fire and sweetness to what we ask for.

Works of money and gain in Quimbanda will always be about luck and chance, as this is the nature of these spirits, and so it is important that we become attentive, follow opportunities opening up and place ourselves in the proper energy as a bond in its own right. With Exu there is really no free lunch, it is all rooted in an interaction and interchange that takes place in the world, and so these spirits help those who know how to help themselves and see the advantage and opportunity when it arrives.

Other works for gain include those related to selling property or getting a good job, and the technology involved is similar. Let us say you want to sell your house. You will then go to Exu Tranca-Ruas with fourteen coins, a bottle of whiskey, a bottle of cachaça, seven cigars and seven candles. You will offer the coins on a plate to him and fill it up with whiskey and cachaça, stating your goal and feeding him with candles and tobacco. This will be done on a Friday, and the next Friday you will remove seven coins as you light seven candles and give him a fresh cigar. You will leave one of the coins at the gate of your house along with some raw tobacco (*fumo de corda*) and a few drops of the whiskey and cachaça offered. You will do the same at six crossroads, leaving seven offerings in all, and then return to your house in such a way that you do not cross the crossroads where you placed the coins and offerings. Arriving to the gate of your house you will offer a fresh coin to the gate, and upon entering the *tronco* you will give two more coins to Tranca-Ruas, nine in all. You will then again state the purpose of your work and promise to give him triple what was given and make a feast in his honour topped with the blood of a rooster.

As you see, this is a working where we literally open the road for spirits so they can be active as agents of attraction in the route where the offerings were made, hence it can be adapted and applied on a great variety of situations.

This being said, works of this type find success only when a person feels truly deserving; the bond encoded in the person doing the work or the person the work is done for is vital for the success. A person feeling undeserving of good fortune will not be able to attract money and gain. Also, when it comes to gambling and luck, in this field my experience is that games of cards, the casino or the horse race are far more effective arenas than the lottery, for instance.

The lottery is bound by its own rules and regulations that do not invite in the touch of spirit, because its randomized ways are not really in any true bond with luck and chance, but rather it is solely about being present in the right moment. This being said, working with Zé Pelintra to get lucky numbers has at times proved successful, but never appears to be of a lasting effect, more temporary, and repetitions seem to be subject to a low rate of success. Such experiments just affirm that works for gain and money with the Exus are related to moving this virtue and attractor around in the field of possibility, where the Lady of Fortune is truly active.

Also, I have found that in terms of any type of working, we rarely give what we don't have, and so a person struggling with

WORKS FOR GAIN AND MONEY

money will usually not be good at ensuring this bond, whilst a beggar might be enormously successful on the simple premise that nothing might be everything. Hence this is a matter of mighty importance to consider when a work is done, be it for oneself or for someone else. Your attitude is truly a key element in workings like this, as it is in workings of true love versus obsession and desire. The more we understand what is going on, the sharper our goal is, and the clearer our understanding of the bonds present is, the greater the success will be, because in this way we will be able to introduce the right virtues from the kingdoms and use the proper spiritual aid along with our own energetic direction in making the work a success.

Everything can be manipulated, but to do so in clever ways is a skill rooted in cunning and connection with spirit. And I say this because the best workings, the better spells, are not the ones known to us, but those that came into being as spirit and Quimbandeiro merge in the aim towards solutions...

In the same way that wealth can be brought, it can also be annihilated, like in the following working.

You will need:
A pomegranate
2 pigeons
Seven chilli peppers
Honey
Seven coins
Fresh cow's dung
Parts of faeces of dog or cat
Gunpowder
Seven black candles

You will call Exu and draw his *ponto* on a small white plate. You will take the name of the target and write it on seven pieces of paper and place one name in each of the chilli peppers. You will then cut out the centre of the pomegranate and place the seven peppers inside together with coins and honey. Offer one pigeon to the pomegranate and take the plate to a desolate place, dig a hole and fill it with dung and faeces, place the plate on top and cover it with gunpowder. Place seven black candles around and then make a track of gunpowder away from the hole so it can be ignited safely. This done, the other pigeon is given to Exu. This will remove prosperity and monetary luck.

Chapter Seventeen
The Fat Evil Eye

Que linda noite, que lindo luar
What a beautiful night, what a beautiful moon
Dona Pomba Gira aqui venha trabalhar
ady Pomba Gira come here to work
Que linda noite, que lindo luar
What a beautiful night, what a beautiful moon
Dona Pomba Gira leva todo o mal pra lá
Lady Pomba Gira takes all evil and take it away

The evil eye is related to the power of fascination, from the Latin *fascinatio*, that described the faculty some people possess to ensnare, charm or intrigue someone, and was consequently in league with the word enchantment, which means a spell as much as to fascinate someone, as we see in terms like being 'spell-bound'. Hence this is a power some people have a natural access to that is bound in the presence of an emotional charge that is released. When speaking of the evil eye we are speaking of negative emotions—and in particular envy and hatred—that are then willingly or unwillingly projected upon a child, household, animals, garden—basically anything can be subject to the effects of the evil eye. The most widespread remedy against the evil eye is the use of spit and curses, followed closely by salt. Effective remedies against it are to spit in the footsteps of the one projecting the evil eye and curse the person to the effect 'may the Devil take so and so', 'may so and so rot in hell, 'may so and so fall prey to their own wickedness and so help me Satan'. Salt thrown at or after the person—or in their footsteps—is another effective remedy if given immediately.

The evil eye is one of the most common sources of misfortune, and can be as strong in effect as if an actual work had been done, because it is a projection of envy, jealousy and nefarious hateful sentiments that is given passage to the target by these wicked sentiments being transferred upon them, willingly or unwillingly. The most important guard we can perform in order to keep this under control is to watch our own capacity for envy and not allow these sentiments to find fertile ground in us. Doing this, the projections of the evil eye will have difficulties generating a bond, due to the anchor of envy not finding solid ground to affix itself into. Spiritual hygiene in the form of weekly herbal baths, fumigations and house washes should be part of one's spiritual routine, and thus as a consequence negative energy and *maleficia* projected willingly or unwillingly will not find a proper atmosphere in which to grow.

There are actually quite few countermeasures of a ritual sort we find in Quimbanda, and the only format for getting rid of the evil eye I have knowledge of is to make a bath of rue/*arruda* (*Ruta graviolens*), lavender/*alfazema* (*Lavandula sp.*), basil/*manjericão* (*Ocimum gratissimum*), with a pinch of pepper, some sulphur and a pinch of sea salt. The bath is then prepared with fresh herbs and presented to your *guia*/Tata. Lights are lit and the situation presented, a generous sip of cachaça is taken and then spit into the bath with an exclamation of the sort 'rid me of this evil'.

The bath is then taken in front of the Exus and allowed to dry for some ten minutes or so. In some cases, the floor of the *tronco* is also washed with this herbal solution—but then a bottle of cachaça is added to the bath for washing. The same can be done in the household if one's entire household and home have become afflicted.

There are on the contrary several countermeasures and protective actions that can be done, most of them involving plants of protection, which is in itself interesting in terms of the bond between fascination/evil eye and the properties of certain plants that naturally break negative sentiments.

The king amongst the breakers of evil eye is Rue, in itself a great purgative and also a remedy for afflictions of the eye when used with care—as it can also give blindness used in excess.

Hence, we can conclude that all plants having some renown for protecting against the evil eye are also plants that can cure the eye or in some cases blind the eye.

Other plants are *comigo-ninguém-pode*, *Dieffenbachia* (the dumbcane), *espada-de-são-jorge* ('St. George's sword'), *Sansevieria trifasciata* (the snake plant or mother-in-law's tongue) and *guiné* ('Guinea'), *pimenteira* (Capsicum annuum), *manjericão* (basil) and *alecrim* (rosemary).

For the Quimbandeiros it is in particular *comigo-ninguém-pode* with its red vines and emerald shiny leaves in a serpentine configuration that is used as a guard and barometer. The plant is simply placed at the front door of the house, and given its sensitivity to energies and presences it will show signs of the evil eye by withering in various levels. This happens immediately after a visit from a person who has thrown the evil eye and thus the situation can be easily remedied by any of the strategies presented so far. St. George's sword and rue are two other alternatives, but in mysterious ways it is only *comigo-ninguém-pode* that has this remarkable property of showing the signs of evil eye being spread. A good option is therefore to have present all these plants at strategic places in one's land or house as they are naturally guards and neutralizers of this vibration.

The effects of the evil eye are felt as a sudden decline in what is good, be it health, income, fertility of land or peace of the house, and as we see from accounts of the evil eye it is usually present when false praise is given, which hides envy. People who wish what you have, that feel you are undeserving of your good fortune, are natural vehicles and portents for this nasty vibration.

If we look at *benzedeiras*, those who are cunning in the art of blessing, they tend to use a combination of twigs of rue or rosemary that are soaked in water slightly salted, then slapped on the face and body of the person afflicted along with a prayer. These prayers usually refer to passages in the Bible where the culprit is meeting his death, real or imaginary, be it about the army of Pharaoh drowning in the waters as the healing water is spread over you, or the culprit drowning in the water of the rue or rosemary.

Seeing the technology involved, we see that it is easy to use, for instance, Exu das Cobras as a force to call upon when a cleaning away of evil eye is to be performed, and a *ponto* or prayer can be developed in the same fashion as what was used by the *benzedeiras*, since this procedure has shown itself to have been efficient many a time.

Another technique is to place mirrors in strategic positions, so they will reflect the guests coming to your house. The simple presence of a mirror 'catching a reflection', will catch what is negative. You might want to wash the mirror in saltwater after every visit, ensuring it doesn't accumulate negative virtues.

Another technique is to show the '*figa*' to the person, either in the face or as the person is leaving; also the hand gesture where the dominant finger and the little finger are erect, forming horns directed towards the envious one, is an effective sign and shares the symbolism of horns being able to kill and project away presences, and we might see in this the mythology of horned animals, be they bulls, rams or goats, and their relation to protection and domination to be vital for understanding how such a bond can be effective.

And so by analogy of bonds we can manufacture a Quimbanda protection vessel in the following way:

- Take a horn of a bull, ram or goat and wash it in cachaça at the *tronco/firmeza* and invite in either your *guia* or another Exu good for protection, like Exu das Cobras which I have a soft spot for when it comes to protection—as I have with Exu do Lodo.
- Gather items important for protection, like many of the herbs listed in this lesson (and present them in a dry form), sulphur, shavings of different kinds of bone, and powder of iron, lead and copper along with a lodestone or magnet.
- Gather some earth from seven crossroads and some earth from your door/gate and place it all in front of the *tronco/firmeza*.

THE FAT EVIL EYE

- Call your court and feed the materials with cigar smoke, add some tobacco, some pepper and some garlic to the mixture along with some sage.
- Draw out the *ponto* of the Exu you want to serve as the protective force and burn it with your cigar, sing his *ponto* and add it to the mixture.
- Leave it all over night, with candles lit, and the next night at nightfall you light three candles and start to fill the horn with the collected materials, murmuring that it is for protection as you also sing the *pontos* of the chosen Exu.
- Seal the horn with the wax from the candles and hand it over your doorway.

An object like this will both neutralize evil eye fast and effectively, and it will warn you against those bringing such things into your home.

Chapter Eighteen
Quimbanda and Healing

Seu Meia-Noite na encruza
Mr. Mid-Night in the Crossroad
Galo canta, gato mia
The rooster craws and the cat miaows
Quem trabalha com Exu
Who work with Exu
Não tem hora, não tem dia
Don't have time, nor the day
Busca sempre a melhoria
Always searching for what is better

Considering that the Kimbundu word 'Quimbanda' (a noun) represents a healer, and seeing how few procedures of healing we find in Quimbanda these days, we need to admit that in this field the Bantu roots have been effectively distanced from what we find in contemporary Quimbanda.

We need to turn to works of Antonio de Alva to find Quimbanda healing arts detailed to some extent, and in many instances the workings he provides us with are rooted in the great vault of sympathetic magic we find amongst the folk practitioners of magic and *benzimentos* in Brazil. Naturally there is also Umbanda, and we can speculate whether the healing arts of the Bantu were not in fact incorporated in Umbanda by the use of fumigations, passes and words of power, as the same elements are found in Bantu-speaking cultures to this day. If so, it would suggest that Zélio in incorporating the African legacy into his creation of Umbanda might have been intrigued by the Bantu healing arts.

If we look closely we find that Quimbanda can heal illness; it can heal the soul, a distorted mind, alcoholism and the threat of death, just as it can heal many other afflictions, usually brought on by wildlife and greenwood.

HEALING WATERS

Magical baths or *amaci* should be a part of any spiritual and magical tradition. After all, we are speaking about the world of matter, so the matter should be at all times in a good state for being worked with and worked by. It is amazing how many problems and difficulties can be solved with the physical and spiritual cleanliness provided by *amaci*. Water and herbs can fortify the soul, ease the mind and agitate the spirit. It is most wise to make water and herbs an integral and indispensable part of the spiritual practice. The way of making the *amaci* follows the same pattern; prayers are said or sung as the herbs are macerated. Certainly, some waters are more complex, but what is needed on a day-to-day basis is quite simple and most benign. Here follows a few healing waters of great efficacy:

Amaci for dispelling ghosts and **kiumbas**
You will make a bath of the following ingredients: sea salt, tobacco (*Nicotiana sp.*), basil (*Ocimum gratissimum*), odundun (*Kallanchoe crenata*), levante (*Mentha viridis*) and petals of white roses.

Amaci for bringing abundance and money
You will use the following ingredients: folha de fortuna (*Kallanchoe pinnata*), honey, cowry shells, basil (*Ocimum gratissimum*), bay laurel (*Laurus nobilis*), leaves of grape (*Vitis sp.*) and leaves, or flesh, of honeydew melon.

Amaci for preparing a working of Quimbanda
You will blend the following ingredients in hot water: cachaça, tobacco (*Nicotiana sp.*), chilli pepper *(Capiscum sp.)*, ginger *(Zingiber officinale)*, and leaves of datura *(Stramonium* or *inoxia)*.

Amaci for restoring strength of soul and will

For this purpose you will make a bath of rosemary (*Rosmarinus sp.*), thyme (*Thymus sp.*), laurel (*Laurus nobilis*), spinach (*Spinacia oleracea*), boldo *(Plectranthus barbatus)* and coconut water.

Amaci for elevation and strength of the mind

You will make the bath with these herbs: levante (*Mentha viridis*), odundun (*Kallanchoe crenata*), anis (*Pimpinella anisum*), cherry (*Prunus serotina*), mulberry (*Morus sp.*), saffron (*Crocus sativus*) and coconut water, making sure that the head is washed very well with these herbs.

Amaci for breaking the evil eye

You will take a bath in the following herbs and also use this as a house wash. The herbs are: espada-de-são-jorge (*Sansevieria trifasciata*), rue *(Ruta graviolens)*, lavender (*Lavandula sp.*) and rosemary (*Rosmarinus sp.*).

HEALING FUMES

Fumigations are important and are ascribed to the influence of *pretos-velhos*, or Old Blacks. Here are given a few traditional blends that are all used in the same manner. You will blend the ingredients together in equal parts and place on burning coals and fumigate the house, especially corners and bathrooms. The ashes will then be given to the four corners of the house.

Fumigation for expelling negativity

You will need rue (*Ruta graviolens*), raw tobacco (*Nicotinia sp.*), barba de velho (*Tillandsia usneoides*), scrapings of a bull horn, lavender (*Lavandula*), myrrh and sugar cane (dried and torn).

Fumigation for exorcising hostile spirits

You will need the skin of garlic, asafoetida (*Ferula asafoetida*), guiné (*Petiveria alliacea*), folha de fogo (*Clidemia sp.*), filings of deer horn, barba de velho (*Tillandsia usneoides*), hair of horse.

Fumigation for bringing good luck to the house

You will need guiné (*Petiveria alliacea*), rue (*Ruta graviolens*), raw tobacco (*Nicotinia sp.*), coffee beans and leaves, brown sugar, cow dung, rosemary (*Rosmarinus sp.*).

Fumigation to expel the Evil Eye

You will need lavender (*lavandula*), rue (*Ruta graviolens*), guiné (*Petiveria alliacea*), rosemary (*Rosmarinus sp.*), Palo Santo or frankincense, laurel (*Laurus nobilis*), benzoin.

The Table of Cure – *a work to heal a sick child*

This work is done with, for instance, Exu Malé or any Exu or Pomba Gira in the kingdom of das Praias. You will need a new white cloth, a plain white cup, a bottle of white or transparent glass, three white roses, water from a stream, and three small white plates. You will take the cloth and cover the table that is used for the working. This must be done with care and genuine interest in effecting a cure. Place the bottle with the river water at one end of the table and the cup at its side. Place here a white candle and three white dishes, one rose in each dish.

The child—or the afflicted one—should be presented to the table in proximity to the items presented. The following prayer should be said over the child:

> *Powerful emissaries of the kingdom of waters*
> *With all my powers and all strength in my heart*
> *I shall transform this water into your medicine*
> *With your blessing this water is now medicine for (state the name of the afflicted one)*
> *With this I greet you and thank you*
> *And I stay firm in my unwavering conviction*
> *So may it be.*

At this point offer up prayers and *pontos* to the Exu chosen to assist the working. The head of the child should be washed in the water and the roses taken to an ocean or river either by the child or in the name of the child petitioning cure and healing. The water should be consumed in equal parts over the course of seven days to effectuate the cure.

As we see, at the root of Quimbanda healing arts we find the intercession of plants, and in this we see that the Quimbandeiro is truly a person who is in deep harmony with what lives in the woods. But as we spoke of before, the woods are where civilization began, and so in learning, understanding and establishing a relationship with these plants and spirits of the forest we will also be able to recognize them in their urban manifestation. One example is *Abre-Caminho*, meaning 'road opener', that translated into a more urban language will be any plant that breaks through concrete or opens a way. Again, let me stress that readymade formulas are solely guidelines; we need to aim towards being guided by spirit itself, because it is in this dance between realms that magic happens and it is in this realm we can effectuate miracles.

CHAPTER NINETEEN

Spirit Houses

Exu fez uma casa
Exu made a house
Sete portas, sete janelas
Seven doors, seven windows
Exu não precisa de casa
Exu don't need a house
É Pomba Gira que vai morar nela
It is Pomba Gira who will live there

The physical vessel that serves as a home or 'body' for Exu and Pomba Gira is called *assentamento*, that is often translated into the meaningless 'settlement' in English. A more accurate translation would be in reference to what is settled being a covenant, agreement, or pact with a spirit in the form of 'seating' the entity in question, to give it a house or a body. The Quimbanda *assentamento* hearkens from the Kongo, Angola and Bantu sorcerous technology where the spirit is assembled in a cauldron or a pot, and there are several varieties to be found as to how to arrange the covenant and its deeper meanings. This is only natural, seeing as this legacy came to Brazil through Cabinda, which was one of the prime ports for deporting slaves from Kongo, Angola and other Bantu-speaking regions. What every procedure of making an *assentamento* has in common, at least to my knowledge, is that the idea is to build a 'house' or a 'body' for the spirit to inhabit, and it is often in this procedure that some differences arise, with elements that are conceived of as essential in some traditions considered less so in others.

Hence the sorcerous technology used in making an *assentamento* is different from what we can find in the Bantu traditions that migrated to Cuba and generated Palo Mayombe, where the equivalent of the *assentamento* is called *prenda* or *nkisi*. That technology involves the creation of a new *nkisi* in body and soul, not only a house or body for an already existing entity to move into. This distinction is important, even if in Palo Kimbisa we find technology more similar to the construction of *assentamentos* than in Palo Mayombe, Monte and Briyumba.

Let us take one example, the elements necessary to make the Spirit House of Exu Morcego, the Bat Exu. We need first of all the correct *ponto riscado*, which in his case is the following:

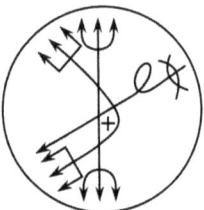

This *ponto riscado* is the signature of Exu Morcego that is marked in the bottom of the vessel, an iron cauldron or a terracotta jar, that will serve as his house or body, which is then activated in secret ways to attract the attention of Exu Morcego. The secret ways consist in items, elements and powders that are placed upon the signature, but also how this is done is important if a proper ignition of the signature is to be made.

The other elements necessary to seat Exu Morcego and make the covenant are the following items:

Earth from a crossroad, earth from the town square, earth from the road, earth from a marketplace, earth from the woods, earth from the cemetery, earth from an avenue, clay stone from a crossroad, one ironwork of the *ponto* of Exu Morcego, seven types of pepper, seven types of Exu herbs, seven types of alcoholic drink (amongst them absinth is essential), palm oil, honey, mercury, sulphur, powder of coal, powder of black *pemba* (chalk), powder of iron, powder of lead, powder of tin, powder of gourd, powder of silver, powder of copper, powder of gold, a magnet, one ruby, one onyx, one crystal, one railroad nail, three horseshoes, twenty-one nails (the type used for coffins or horseshoes), twenty-one coins, twenty-one cowry shells, 1 knife, the following seven beans and seeds: Fava de Exu (Exu bean), Olho de Boi (Bull's eye), Olho de Pombo (Eye of Pigeon), Garra de Exu (Claw of Exu), Olho de Cabra (Eye of Goat), Figo do Diabo (Devil's liver), Olho do Lobo (Wolf's eye), broken glass, barbed wire, the head of a poisonous snake, 1 scorpion, 1 bat (preferably alive). You will also need a goat and three roosters to seal the pact.

As you see, there are many elements that need to be in place, and there is a certain order to how the elements are placed inside to make a perfect body or perfect house. And of course, no listing of ingredients that you find in a book or online will be complete, there will always be elements needed due to the nature of the relationship between the Tata and the Exu or Pomba Gira which are essential to seal the covenant. This means that just throwing the elements together on a solitary basis like an amateur chef following with rigour the recipe in the cookbook will not achieve the presumed goal.

A simpler form of Spirit House would be one for the *malandros*, the hustlers, represented by Zé Pelintra and Maria Navalha. This would be akin to building a force field recognized by the hustler spirits like Zé Pelintra.

Quite simply you will take a terracotta jar, wash it in cachaça, then draw his *ponto riscado* in the bottom with red and white *pemba* (chalk), like we see in the *ponto* above. To this is added a razor, a deck of cards, seven dice, a game of dominoes, seven daggers or knives, a small vase (*quartinha*) of porcelain or terracotta, seven large white cowry shells and 7 brown African cowry shells. Finally a statue of Zé Pelintra and/or Maria Navalha is included, and this vessel can then be worked by the aid of offering cachaça, cognac, cigars and candles together with song and petition to bring good fortune and protection to dwell in your home. A vessel like this will not be a covenant, it doesn't mean that you have seated Zé Pelintra, as in order to do that it is necessary to generate something similar to his body as well.

Another option for bringing in these entities closer through a physical vessel is to actually build a house for them, which in practical terms can mean refurbishing and painting a cabinet where you gather meaningful and sacred items to populate the house, such as statues, items found in places important for the Exu and/or Pomba Gira in question, as well as their cups and patuás (charms/talismans). The house is then worked by the aid of songs, candles, drinks and tobacco.

Yet another way of building a closer relationship with these spirits through a physical house is what I call the devotion vessel. This vessel will serve as a focal point for a gradual build-up of the presence of Exu. This is a simple and harmless way of building connection as there is no covenant or pact involved. To make a devotion vessel for Pomba Gira you need the following:

> A vessel, preferably of copper, terracotta or porcelain
> Seven coins
> Seven cowry shells
> Seven pieces of rose quartz
> Seven pieces of crystal
> One piece of onyx
> Dried rose petals
> One lipstick
> One bottle of perfume

The vessel is washed in cachaça or champagne, and this being done the items are gathered inside.

To make a devotion vessel for Exu you will need the following:

A vessel, preferably of iron, terracotta or porcelain
Seven cowry shells
Seven African (large brown) cowry shells
Seven pieces of obsidian
Seven pieces of onyx
One crystal
Tobacco
Black pepper
Red pepper
A small knife

As for Pomba Gira, the vessel is washed in cachaça prior to adding the elements. Over time, items that seem proper to give a particular quality or flare to the vessel are added. If the vessel is for Pomba Gira Cigana, do add a deck of cards or a beautiful hand fan to the vessel. If the vessel is for Exu Sete Catacumbas, you will want to add seven stones or pebbles from seven different places in the cemetery to ensure that the quality of the vessel is in harmony with the power you seek to align it with.

The form of Exu or Pomba Gira that we aim towards manifesting through constructing a devotion vessel is one by which Exu or Pomba Gira slowly develops into a guide, a tutelary spirit, which is the most important work possible to do. The connection or bond with the Exu and/or Pomba Gira wanting to work with you is what makes Quimbanda powerful and living. Hence, in my opinion, making the full covenant and having your spirit guide seated in both 'body' and 'house' is not a commitment most people should undertake, as the pact, the covenant, is a marriage with no recourse for divorce.

And in how the *assentamentos* are made we can also see the root of the succession of Quimbanda. For instance, in Umbanda it is common to receive *quartinhas* containing various secrets and precious stones washed in herbs as the '*assentamento*' of Exu or Pomba Gira, with a *ferramenta* (*ponto* forged in metal) flanking the *quartinha*. A Quimbanda *assentamento* proper is made from earth, stone, woods and herbs as its most important components. Arthur

Ramos writes about how the *nkisi* was seated in his discourse on 'Fetishism of the Bantus' in Brazil in his 1940 publication, *O Negro Brasileiro*, suggesting that the Angola, Bantu and Kongo legacy appears to have been largely maintained in the construction of the spirit pots as we find in the construction of the *assentamentos* of Exu and Pomba Gira today.

The idea behind a Quimbanda *assentamento* is to build a seat or house for a given power to rest upon or within. It is not a spirit prison, but a home. On the contrary, in Palo Mayombe it is said that the construction of the spirit pot is to make the world of the spirit. Not to say that these two ideas mutually exclude one another, but we are speaking of Quimbanda and how the Bantu legacy took shape in Brazil, which means that we are not building a world, but the body of the spirit itself. Surely we find these ideas in pure Mayombe, which is in itself interesting, but let us leave it at that so we don't mix the planes to much and end up seeing the one as the other, because the truth is that a root produces a tree, but on the trunk that grows from this root we will have many branches.

The *assentamento* is a careful gathering of items that holds powers that attract the spirit we want to make a home for. The home, offered tobacco, alcohol and blood, will then 'seat' the spirit in its house. And here in this simplicity we find the complexity, because everything we use in this process is *nkisi*. Our breath and our energy, the items, animal, mineral and vegetal, are *nkisi*, as is the spirit we seek to attract. This means that the ready product, the Spirit House we made, will always be a unique expression, a meeting between our force and determination and the spirit we are seating. This composite is *nkisi*, 'an object of power'.

If we look at Angola and the district known as Congo, we see that everything that demonstrably holds some power is *nkisi*, be it a crucifix, a tree struck by lightning, a stone that emits something odd, birds with their song and behaviour, all reveals that we are living in a world saturated with powers.

And so, for a Bantu-man, a Jesuit with his cross being able to command the masses is holding *nkisi*. This has nothing to do with religion or race, culture or dogma. It is about an open realization of the existence of power wherever power is found.

This attitude invites in a complete breakdown of anything religiously loaded, where we seek the object of power charged with the power it holds, discarding the route towards this power. In the same way as we know a tree struck by lightning holds the power of lightning, we also know that the crucifix holds a commanding power. We don't care about the mythology of thunder and lightning or the Christian religion and dogmas, we see an object of power—and any object that holds power we can take and use for other purposes, like attracting a spirit that is in resonance with the power we see in the empowered object.

Chapter Twenty
Living Quimbanda

Abre a porta no teu mundo
Open the gates in your world
E deixa esse povo entrar
And allow these people to enter
O Exu é um povo amigo
Exu is a friendly people
Ele só quer te ajudar
He only seek to help
Eu tô cantando, eu tô louvando
I am singing, I am saluting
Eu tô pedindo a proteção
I am asking for protection
A esse povo de Exu
Ah this people of Exu
Meu camarada, meu irmão
My companion, my brother

Quimbanda is a cult where we interact with spirit head-on through possession and trance states, but it is also a cult that is pragmatic, practical and is engaging with the world where all forms of human and spiritual activity are to be found. In truth, the altar of Exu is every crossroad imaginable. It is possible to commune with this entity in a physical crossroad at night, offering a cigarette, a coin and perhaps a splash of rum, and just waiting, just as in the tales where the Devil is summoned at the crossroad and, this done, one waits for what is coming. To live with Exu, to make one's Quimbanda living, means that wherever you are, your Exu is, hence the candles, the cigarette, the glass of cachaça is offered as an amplifier to what is already there. This can be given at the tavern, in the crossroad, in any place of choice and field of need. The goal should be as the Brazilian adage imparts, that mastery is when you simply throw a bottle of cachaça on the ground and up comes the Devil. The Devil comes because the bond made, the connection made, is solid. In this relationship we can at times be tricked. Sometimes these spirits trick us so we can get humble in life, just as they were humbled in life during their incarnations. In this way they serve as models for how we should understand that beautiful and secret union we know as a pact, to be executed in ways workable and full of effect and results. Sometimes the trickery happens because that's who they are and for whatever reasons—and the reason can often be that they see we need to loosen up, laugh and not take life so darn serious.

Quimbanda is about understanding crossroads, understanding that every situation is a meeting between memory and the present and here comes choices, and our spirit guides can aid us in making better choices, because Exu and Pomba Gira quite often became who they are through bad choices. This means that in taking them on as guides in life, we do invite death in, but a mirthful death who knows that life is just a journey towards him…

Walking with Death as our guide can be challenging for many, but so can the implicit challenge of fire in Quimbanda. The sacraments offered are all fiery, be it the intensity of emotion, the illusion of power and control, the peppers, the entire dungeon of vices and impulses repressed or embraced, or the most indispensable and important parts of the cult, the alcohol and the tobacco.

Tobacco has a long history of sacred and recreational use but can also, as we know, lead to addiction and illness and is, as alcohol, an example of how everything offered to Exu should by humans be taken in moderation. Speaking of tobacco, we have the way the cigarette was presented through the Marlboro Man and Coco Chanel, recommended by doctors to ease stress. One of the more intense sacramental uses of tobacco must be found amongst the Warao tribe in the Venezuelan part of the Amazon forest. Within the beautiful and intricate vision of creation held by this tribe we find the owner of the western gate called Hoebo, the Ancient One, who rules over the land of darkness. In his realm there are only two small lights, one white and the other yellow, that cast a bone-white illumination over his kingdom. In the very place where the Sun starts its descent is found a house. In this house lives Miana, which is the soul of Hoebo. Miana is dependent upon drinking blood from a cosmic blood duct to keep strong, and is the guardian of what Johannes Wilbert calls 'dark shamanism' and 'assault sorcery'. Of interest in regard to the tobacco is that the cult of Hoebo and Miana is a vampiric cult where tobacco is absolutely indispensable. Actually, the older initiates do tend to become yellow, the colour of tobacco, to be permanently in the same frequency as Miana. To give an idea of the importance of tobacco for this cult occupied with death, spirits of the woods, hostile spirits, death and all things that move in the troubled waters beneath the human existence, the neophyte will undertake a sojourn where he is fasting but smoking incessantly. As Wilbert writes:

> Toward the end of this initial period, the master takes the burning end of a two-foot-long cigar into his mouth and blows a hoebo spirit into it. He hands this magically endowed cigar to his anxious ward and asks him to inhale it deep into his chest. On performing the same task for a second time (...), the student levitates in narcotic trance to the zenithal house, where he comes face-to-face with Miana's son, Hoebo, the guardian of dark shamanism... Chances are that the drug transports him deeper into Miana's world, the neophyte experiences tobacco amblyopia (dimness of vision) and colour blindness, which allows him to discern only white and yellow. His world takes on a bone-white silverish hue, and he sees better in crepuscular light than in the open sunshine.[18]

In addition to how the Warao see tobacco as a sacrament intimately linked to the world beneath the western gate, the land

---

18 2004: pp. 36–37.

of darkness, death and sorcery, it is also interesting to see that the world view of the Warao is strikingly similar to the Bantu-Kongo cosmology that for the novice in the mysteries of tobacco is a journey of tempering fire, mastering pain and contemplating death, similar to both the approach towards these mysteries adopted by Saiva followers, Aghoris, and what is found in the inner dimensions of Quimbanda.

Alcohol shares similar dark features as tobacco, where excess opens up to darkness, the demonic and the obsessive. These forces are often called *kiumbas*, similar to larvaes, and would take the form of hungry ghosts, desperate souls and quite often they remind of the descriptions we find of ghouls in Middle-eastern myths. Ghouls or Al'Ghoul is a class of djinn which is a species of being created from smokeless fire, found in ruins, cemeteries and in the wilderness, that would attack people and feast on their flesh. Ghouls were associated with gluttony and greed. It is tempting to embrace the erroneous etymology that creates a relationship between *al'ghoul* and alcohol, but rather the root of ghoul, 'gal' means 'to cast spells' and 'wrath'; also the Akkadian *gallu*, which was a Mesopotamian class of hostile chthonic spirits associated with misfortune and destruction of luck, might be brought in here for an etymological similarity at least. Renaissance medicine in Europe followed in the tradition of Galen who saw depression and dark temperaments as a product of accumulation of bile, which in turn was caused by excess of alcohol or food. This condition called melancholy was ruled over by Saturn and reveals a resonance between gluttony, anger, fire and Saturn that is the theme of Quimbanda, for good and for bad. The drunkard and chain-smoker are always potential mediums in the right circumstances, as Exu takes shape in the fiery fog of the tobacco and the fiery water of the cachaça, hence paraphrasing Charles Bukowski: 'what matters most is how well you walk through the fire' can surely be an anthem of Quimbanda.

The last thing important to address in the practical arsenal of Quimbanda is oracles. The primordial oracle is spirit itself, but we shall not be so naïve that we don't look aside for the possibility of spirit at times lying. It is important to constantly remember what type of spirit we are dealing with and the proximity we have with the Exus and Pomba Giras. Allegories speaking of distance and proximity in human relationships work very well transposed upon Exu and Pomba Gira. Let us take a couple of examples to give a better idea. An interesting person moves in next door to you, you find out that he is a drug kingpin and you want to purchase some of his product. Do you simply go there, knock on his door, shovel some cash in his face and ask what you want, or do you introduce yourself first and approach him calmly and respectfully? Another example can be going to the bank demanding a loan. Do you come with the despair of a beggar, do you come with honesty and integrity, or do you come with the attitude of a wise guy? Each attitude will give you a different response, and it is the same way with Exu and Pomba Gira; the way you approach them is important for the reaction and relationship to be established. Hence in the process of establishing this solid relationship it is good to have recourse to an oracle, and whilst Pomba Gira Cigana responds well to the use of cards, especially playing cards and Lenormand, the four shells are a simple and precise oracle that can be used to affirm doubts and likewise affirm answers to questions. You will need four cowry shells, preferably the brown African ones, and you will remove the belly of the shell, so you have one natural opening, the shell's mouth, and one opening that is artificial, its belly. The mouth talks, the belly doesn't, hence four shells with the belly up will not talk and this is interpreted as a 'no', because the answer is veiled in darkness, still in the womb, which gives another dimension to the quality of the negative reply. These shells are washed in a solution of cachaça (or rum), martini rosso and whiskey where seven chilli peppers, a pinch of cemetery earth and tobacco are added. You will steep the shells in this fluid for three days, making sure that a seven-day candle is lit during these seventy-two hours. This simple consecrating of the shells will give you an oracle that is in tune with the energetic presence of Exu and Pomba Gira.

When using the shells, they are shaken in both hands in front of the effigy or on the *ponto riscado* of the entity in question as the following is recited:

Mojuba o Exu/Pomba Gira (NN) /x 3
Ask your question, the simpler the better.
Laroyê

The shells are thrown and the pattern interpreted in accordance with the configurations in the photo below:

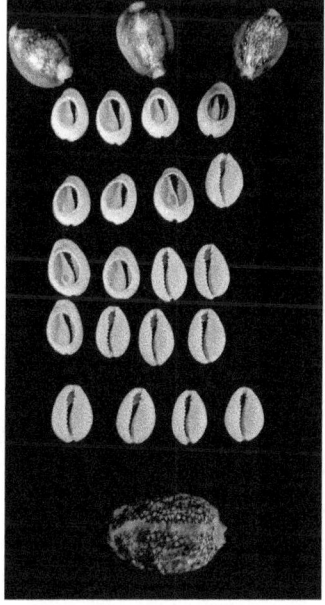

The responses from top to bottom:

I   No, very negative, ask again, rephrase the question
II A negative outcome, rephrase the question
III Yes, balanced, good, positive outcome
IV Yes, but... something is lacking or amiss, rephrase the question
V   Yes, strong, positive; some would interpret it as too positive, excessive

Chapter Twenty-one
Calunga

Eu vou girar
I will spin
Eu vou girar
I will swirl
E na minha caminhada
And as I walk on
Vou passar pelo Encruzo
I will pass through the 'Cruzeiro'
E na minha caminhada
And as I walk on
Na Calunga eu vou ficar
In the Calunga is where I will stay

Calunga is the watery division between worlds, specifically the surface of the ocean that is both a mirror and an entrance. Entering beneath this mirror we are submerged in liquid space and we find here the stars reflecting themselves in the mysterious abysmal waters, the perpetual darkness that holds the seeds of all becoming.

The ocean holds the idea of mystery, the unknown; it is where the *kisimbi* copulates in moist caves found at the ocean shore to bring forth mermaids and mermen reputed to teach their children the secrets of clairvoyance, prophecy, dreaming and other secret and mystical technologies. The *kisimbi* represents both ancestry and mystery, and speaks of how we are all connected to everything in various ways, depending on our station in life and the bonds we have managed to establish. More precisely the *kisimbi* represents the original inhabitants of a place, forces of nature that resided in objects like stones, roots, plants, sand and waters, that when brought from Africa to Brazil had to generate a new sequence of spiritual forces from where they were planted. The *kisimbi* was important both for *bakulu*, or ancestors, and the *minkisi* as a living, serpentine and mercurial power that was responsible for the accumulation, growth and transformation of spiritual forces, a function we find within Exu and Pomba Gira nowadays.

The idea of time for the Kongo sorcerer is like the Calunga; it is a state, everchanging with depths and mysteries, a spiral and not a line. In the Kongo nation of Haitian Vodou we find the deeper idea of Calunga represented by the *Lwa Eritaj Kongo Bó Lanmè*, meaning 'The Truthful Hunter from the Good Ocean'. This lwa, as all Kongo lwa, is offered both *klerin*, sugarcane distillate, and *assorossi*, a drink prepared from bitter melon (*Momordica sp.*), in memory of how existence on this side of the ocean mirror is always strong, intoxicating, but also astringent, as it was in the Trans-Atlantic.

The process of becoming memory is found in the ocean. A body is thrown into the ocean, the body dismantles and becomes a part of the ocean. The bones, once white, become yellow until they evaporate and become calcium, making up part of this liquid space of memories. The ocean is memory and it is *ndozi*, dream. It represents beginnings, ends and transformations. In the *Calunga pequena*, the Little Calunga, or cemetery, similar mysteries are replicated, especially the transformation of the body and bones, and of a person entering into the soil becoming part of the memory of the cemetery.

The three vital crossroads of Quimbanda are the Calunga, the Cruzeiro and the Encruzilhada or Crossroad, in a rhythm where the entity surges from the wet or mouldy realms of the Calunga and through an axis of ascent represented by the Cruzeiro. The Cruzeiro is the central cross in the Catholic cemetery where candles and offerings are given to the ancestors. This place, usually at the centre of the cemetery, is where we find the access and departure point both literally and symbolically for the spirits to spread out into the world. These Cruzeiros can be understood as large crossroads that attract large gatherings of souls, like for instance in roadside chapels erected at places where people suffered untimely death. These places are potential Cruzeiros, beacons in the world that attract large numbers of souls. From the Calunga and/or the Cruzeiro, Exu and Pomba Gira spread out in the world, like a network of nodes, knots and crossroads affirming myriad powers spread out in the visible and invisible world. The deeper dimensions of Quimbanda are beautiful and intricate, the work itself hard, direct, demanding, yet quite simple, as spirit is worked head-on with dirty feet, muddy hands and the mouth full of smoke and rum.

Quimbanda is full of depth and revelation, and is a cult that never stands still, but is always in flux and reflux, like the waves beating back and forth bringing high tide and low tide, each with its mysteries and changes over time. Since the turn of the twenty-first century there has been a gradually increasing interest in Quimbanda, to understand the cult of Exu on its own premises. These movements came partly from the houses of macumba in Rio de Janeiro and Bahia, but also through Umbanda and Candomblé that in the 1960s saw a stronger tendency towards cultivating Exu and Pomba Gira in their own right. We can see this in how Exu became autonomous in the south of Brazil due to the work and prestige of mediums like Mãe Ieda de Ogum in Porto Alegre and Mãe Cacilda de Assis, from Rio de Janeiro, who made Exu Sete Encruzilhadas, Rei da Lira famous all over Brazil in the 1960s and 70s. In fact, the 1950s to 1970 was a rich period for mediums in Brazil, and it is interesting that it was Exu, as the healer of the people, who took the centre stage. In both these situations, Exu took shape through Candomblé and found its own unique form that led to Quimbanda de Cruzeiro e Almas in the south of Brazil rising to be its sown marvellous cult of Exu, different from Quimbanda in Rio or in São Paulo, which again presents variations of itself, which we must understand reflects the very essence of the feverish mercury spinning at the core of Exu's soul.

Just as the cult of Exu was preserved through Candomblé, so it was through Umbanda. Umbanda managed to preserve a great number of streams of Quimbanda under its all-embracing wings, such that Exu was always taken care of in ways separate from the others. In this process a great number of diverging visions concerning Exu surfaced but what we see in the history of Umbanda is that everything begins and ends with Exu. For instance, if a *gira* of Umbanda is made, small or large, the first thing that is done is to offer *paô* (sea salt, cachaça and candle) to Exu. The last thing that is done is to thank Exu, often with another candle ensuring that his candle is the first and the last.

In the same way, in the sequence of pacts that composes the initiatic road of an Umbanda priest or priestess, the last pact is with Exu, and it is Exu that gives the future father or mother of saint autonomy. This ceremony, however, is very different from all ten previous initiations or pacts preserving the memory of the cult of Exu being something 'other'.

Several houses of Umbanda that are 'raiz', or 'of the root', can be seen as true continuations of macumba and *cabula* where Exu and Pomba Gira have their place side by side with *caboclos* and *pretos-velhos*.

In closing this chapter, one Exu might illustrate the nerve and beauty in what at times can be experienced as confusing in Quimbanda, namely the very identity of these Tatas we call Exu—in this case Exu Marabá. This is an Exu considered quite dangerous, connected to dreams and madness, but he is also an Exu that without mercy kills whatever stands in his way if that is his task, hence at times he is seen as an Exu that takes on some qualities of Ogum and can be depicted as a Roman soldier, similar to St. Expedite. Marabá is also known as Exu Meia-Lua, Exu Half Moon, connected to the lunar phases, but more than this he is an Exu that knows secrets, including the secrets of how life begins and ends through the lunar phases, and has a strong attraction to funerals, especially the part where the corpse is veiled. Quite interestingly, in the coast of Loango, not far from Cabinda which was the prime port for departure of slaves from the Kongo region, we find the famous *nkisi* Maramba that was for some syncretized with St. Lazarus, being a *nkisi* of healing, resurrection and prophesy because he knows many secrets and thus would be able to predict auspicious times. Maramba was also considered to have a violent streak when pushed, as he was also the *nkisi* that warriors would swear oaths to.

Maramba is also a Tupi word for the bushy tree *Eugenia marambaiensis*, that in folklore is said to be inhabited by a child-eating creature known as the Tutu, from the Kimbundu '*quitutu*', meaning ogre, singing lullabies in the moon-lit night to seduce and enthral children. When we look at the *ponto riscado* of Marabá, on the right (below), we see that his qualities are very similar to what is given to Exu Omulu, on the left.

Exu Omulu is syncretised with St. Lazarus, with the exception that for Marabá the mystery of the coffin is even more central, suggesting that the role of Maramba as St. Lazarus is encoded in the *ponto* of Marabá, who is the chief for the people of the soul that is present at the funeral wake. We also find the symbol of the moon in Marabá's *ponto riscado*, a memory of how he is connected through the moon to prophecy, the birth/death cycles and the lullabies of the Tutu hunting for children in the night.

Quimbanda is about this legacy, about words spelt wrong, said wrong, ideas misunderstood, concepts misrepresented that are then transformed through the amoral mercury that flows through Exu into meaning, puzzle and intrigue. Quimbanda is what stirs in the Calunga as memory and mirror, it is about putting your hand through the liquid mirror and taking on Death as your guide in life.

Appendix I
Approaching the Entity

In this appendix some orientations in how to approach an entity will be presented, how to welcome the spirits into your life and how to commune with them. We have chosen a select court of Exus and Pomba Giras to serve as examples. Yet, Quimbanda is at its heart simple and hard. If the connection is good, you will really only need some tobacco, some light, and some alcohol offered in any of the myriad crossroads or kingdoms we find these marvellous entities. Fifteen entities from the most varied kingdoms are used to exemplify how the approach, items, vibration and work is done depending on where and with whom we seek to commune.

Approaching and working with Exu Omolu

Approaching Exu Omolu, you will prepare a simple *padê* for him that consists of manioc flour stirred over the heat with cachaça or similar; when it is reaching the consistency of a porridge you place it in a vessel and stir in red peppers (they can be dried). Then you will add unsalted popcorn to the *padê* and top it with a raw pork steak with vinegar and palm oil poured over.

If you want to add a special touch to it you will take a red onion, cut off the top and peel it from the inside in such a way that you are left with an onion cup. You then take a pineapple and you do the same, cut off the top and remove the fruit meat so you are left with a pineapple cup. In the pineapple you offer white wine and in the onion cup you offer cachaça. If you don't do this, two ordinary cups are good enough. You will then offer the drinks to him with three white candles and one black along with a good cigar. This can be done in front of his effigy or directly on his *ponto* drawn on the floor with white *pemba*.

You will then sing to him with the following *pontos*:

Omolu aê atotó, Ele é Exu!
Omolu aê atotó, Ele é Exu!

Se Ele corre os quatro cantos	*If he runs to the four corners*
Quatro cantos sem parar	*Four corners without rest*
Se Ele corre os quatro cantos	*If he runs to the four corners*
E pra seus filhos ajudar	*It is to help his children*
Salve Seu Omolu!	*Salutations to Mr. Omolu!*

This *ponto* being sung three times or more will generate an atmosphere where communion can take place, but it is also possible to ascend upon this and invite him in as an intercessor with your ancestors.

Using him as a mediator for connecting with your ancestors you will present a cup of white wine, a cup of cachaça, a cup of coffee and a cup of water, but you will make a cross using seven candles, dominated by white candles but also some black, seven in total. You will then place one of the cups at the end of each arm of the cross made from candles (doesn't matter where you place what, but west is water, north is coffee, south is cachaça and east is white wine if such orientations are helpful in your practice).

You can use the same *pontos* as in the welcome, and then you will tell him, when you sense him, the following:

Owner of the Cruzerio
Lord of all the People of the Cemetery
Master of the Midnight

APPENDIX I: APPROACHING THE ENTITY

Listen to me as I ask you to open tombs
And graves, mausoleums and
Sepulchres to give voice to my ancestral blood

Sing again his *ponto*, or just *Omolu aê atotó, Ele é Exu!* over and over again until you feel slightly dizzy. You will then start to call your ancestors by name, and as you do so you will dip your fingers on the left hand in each of the cups and sprinkle some of the contents at the centre of the cross.

Recite each ancestral name at least three times, if you sense something is showing up, but is slow to come, keep on naming them. At the end of the naming of the ancestors you will stay quiet in the presence of Omolu and your ancestors and be attentive without forcing anything.

When you are done, softly extinguish all the candles except for one white that you will leave to burn down by itself. The liquids can be disposed of the night after, preferably on the earth itself, but as the virtues are gone there is nothing wrong in throwing them in the sink either.

Approaching Exu Capa Preta
Exu Black Cape

There are several ways of approaching this Exu and welcoming him to your *firmeza*, and the simple variant is to offer him seven candles in the colours red and black—with a predominance of black—offer up a generous glass of aguardiente, cachaça or whiskey, and sing or play his *pontos* while a cigar, lit and the fumes spreading over his image, is offered up. As a first encounter, playing recorded *pontos* is perfectly fine. Then you stay in this atmosphere generated by inviting in the spirit.

If you want to gain further goodwill and benefit from the spirit you will do the following:

Get a black cloth and with white chalk you will draw his *ponto*. Make a circle of seven black candles around the *ponto*, and in the centre you will offer him boiled black beans, heavy on the pepper, red and black varieties. A small knife or dagger is placed there, and seven pieces of beef fried lightly in palm oil on both sides (i.e. they will still be raw inside) is placed on top. Cachaça or aguardiente is offered on top of this, both on the meat and in a separate glass, as well as cigarillos and cigars. Exu Capa Preta also likes scented cigarillos or tobaccos, so these can also be offered, and likewise a small portion of some sweet liquor can be added to this as well. His *ponto cantado* is then given, one example of which is the following:

Com faca de dois gumes	With a double-edged blade
Não convém brincar	it is not pertinent to fool around
É o Exu da Capa Preta	And this Exu Black Cape
Vamos respeitar	Let us respect
Exu do Capa Preta	Exu of the Black Cape

Stay with the spirit as the atmosphere is building, partake of the alcohol and cigars—or bring your own cup and cigar—but in moderation, at least at first, because you are aiming at communion and not being overtaken by the spirit. Leave the session with a token of gratitude, respectfully, when you feel the time is right.

Let the candles burn down by themselves, and the day after you will tie the cloth around the collected offerings and bring it to a park or similar and dispose of this in a hidden place, preferably close to or at the roots of some old tree.

Approaching Exu Chama Dinheiro
Exu Drawing in Money

To placate this Exu in your home you will locate the place in your house where money and opportunity is generated. This means, if you have a home office, he will be there, if the kitchen is found to be a creative realm, he will be placed there. He will be placed on ground level on a plate in the form of his effigy or other proper items, which are then placed on his *ponto riscado*.

You will preferably choose Friday, Saturday or Monday to greet him, and approach him by offering to him a glass of red wine, cigarillos (which can very well be scented) and three candles, either three white ones or one white, one black and one red. In addition, you will offer him fruits, figs, apples and peaches, and in each of the fruits you will insert a dime. Make the offering to him singing the following *ponto*:

Sala, salá mucalero,	*Sala, salá mucalero,*
Sala Lebará e sala	*Sala Lebará e sala,*
Saravá Seu Pedra Negra,	*Saravá Mr Pedra Negra,*
Sala munganga ê sala,	*Sala munganga ê sala,*
Não sei o que faço,	*I don't know what to do,*
Não sei o que resolver,	*I don't know what to decide,*
Estou para morrer,	*I am about to die,*
Exu Chama Dinheiro,	*Exu Drawing in Money,*
Vem me ajudar,	*Come to help me,*
Faz entrar dinheiro,	*Make money manifest,*
Para me salvar	*To save me*

Leave the candles to burn out by themselves, and the morning after you will remove the dimes from the offerings and place them around him on his plate. You will take one sip of the wine and the rest will be poured over the fruits.

This should be done before brushing teeth or showering. Leave it there along with one candle lit. Go and take a shower, dress up in good clothes and use perfume and scent. You will then collect the offerings in a bag of some sort and leave it at a 'crossroad of money'—this can be a variety of places, but naturally close to a bank or a successful enterprise is good.

The offering doesn't have to be left on the ground, but can also be disposed of in a trash can at the crossroad or kingdom. If you do this, say:

'*May the Mulambos take my petition. Salve os Mulambos. Laroyé.*'

If the petition yields small results or the results are delaying, repeat the procedure three more times, but add to this strong peppers and strong alcohol—and if possible, gunpowder that is ignited at the end of the petition.

Another *ponto* that can be used is one that begs the inclusion of sea sand and white sea shells on its plate of offering; the *ponto* is as follows:

Eu fui na beira do mar	I went to the shore of the ocean
Fui só pra ver exu girar	I went just to see Exu moving around
Seu Marabô e Maré no Seu Cruzeiro	Mr. Marabó is like the tide in His crossroad/place of power
Vem pra saudar um Exu	Came to greet an Exu
Chama Dinheiro	Calling for Money in
Seu Cruzeiro	His crossroad/place of power
Vem pra saudar um Exu	Came to greet an Exu
Chama Dinheiro	Calling for Money
Buscando riquezas no mar	Searching for wealth in the ocean
Fui só pra ver exu girar	I went just to see Exu move around

APPENDIX I: APPROACHING THE ENTITY

Eu fui na beira do mar	*I went to the shore of the ocean*
Fui só pra ver exu girar	*I went just to see Exu moving around*
Seu Marabô e Maré no	*Mr. Marabó is like the tide in*
Seu Cruzeiro :I	*His crossroad/place of power*
Vem pra saudar um Exu	*Came to greet an Exu*
Chama Dinheiro :I	*Calling for Money*
Buscando riquezas no mar	*Searching for wealth in the ocean*
Fui só pra ver exu girar	*I went just to see Exu move around*

Approaching Exu Curadôr
Exu the Healer

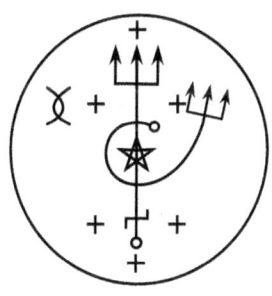

Exu Curadôr is a healer and a medicine man, the typical *curandeiro*. He holds a special relationship with Exu Meia-Noite and they can be favourably worked together.

He can be given cigars and cachaça mixed with honey as offerings. The pipe filled with leaves of nettles and datura can be used by his mediums when they wish to be mounted—the pipe is in general the greatest vehicle for summoning him. He looks like a *preto-velho*, but his eyes shift from red to green, and because of this some say he was an African shaman and witch. He always carries a bag to collect his herbs and smoking blends, and at times he is seen with his companion Pomba Gira Curadôr, a mistress of seduction and sensual gastronomy. This Exu is a calm, yet hot spirit. His name, Curadôr, reflects back on the tradition of *curandeiros* in Brazil. Originally these were wise men and women of African ancestry who knew how to use herbs for ill and good. They could also control animals and were said to possess such insight into nature that they were able to dominate birds and reptiles. Over time these mysteries were fused with European knowledge, but whether the origins were Christian or African, herb work remained the vehicle of healing. This Exu drinks cachaça mixed with honey and/or spices and herbs.

You will welcome him by presenting for him a vessel of a variety of dry herbs, preferably medicinal, but also useless weeds must be present. On this bed of herbs you will offer tobacco, a piece of some animal fur if possible, and a pipe. At the edges of the herbal dish present a few peppers, making a triangular shape that you pour some honey over. Candles, red and black—or in his case white, or white and black—are always placed in odd number sequences (1, 3, 5, 7, 9). In front of the vessel, you place a glass of cachaça or similar and a glass of honey, smoke his pipe, light a cigar and welcome him with his *pontos*; a couple of examples are here:

Em terreiro de Umbanda,	In the terreiro of Umbanda,
Exu vem saravá,	Exu comes to salute,
Se Preto-velho é doto,	If Old Black is a doctor,
Eu é Exu curadô.	I am Exu that heals and cures.

Boa noite, meu senhor,	Good night my lord,
Exu no reino chegou,	Exu at the kingdom has arrived,
Vamos louvar nossa Quimbanda,	Let's praise our Quimbanda,
Viva Exu que é curadô!	Hail Exu that is the Healer!

The day after, you will reduce the herbal offering into dust by drying it in the oven, and gather it around him or into a sachet that you place at his foot together with the pipe. You will draw out the *ponto* on the right side, burn it to ashes and add it to the sachet. Doing this you will

have a basic patuá or charm for healing, and also an increase of herbal intuition which can facilitate rapport with the green realm. Next time you offer him anything—it can be a simple *padê*, just make sure that honey, cachaça and some combination of spices are present in the *padê*—you will top it with a piece of raw meat, preferably of goat; if that is not possible, bovine meat is fine.

Approaching Exu Malé

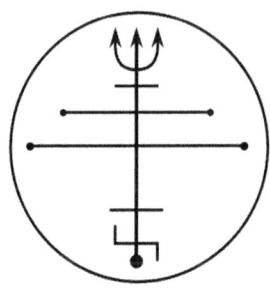

Exu Malé is an old Exu that holds enormous amounts of wisdom from West, Central and North Africa. The name, Malé, is a memory of the Malé people in Rio de Janeiro at the turn of the century. The Malé people were essentially Muslim Ifá practitioners that moved into the urban populations following the slave revolt of the Malé in 1835. Exu Malé is a great Exu to approach for those who do not know the identity of their Exu and Pomba Gira, as he is an Exu quite helpful and compassionate in his strictness. This Exu is said to be of a fluid constitution, and manifests as a *preto-velho* dressed in white, with a white beard. This Exu is a true witch and knows how to work roots and conjure. In Exu Malé is found a great reservoir of African witchcraft and sorcery. He is good at dissolving spells and bindings, and he is one of the most useful spirits for making *despachos*. He smokes a pipe and drinks cachaça and any type of wine. He is also deeply related to the powers of the moon, and one would do well to observe her phases when working with him. He is also said to be an expert in constructing the *ngangas* or spirit vessels of the Kongolese. In this he often uses the assistance of Exu Ganga. Exu Malé is himself a spirit of comfort in the kingdom of the Harp and is the confidant of Exu dos Infernos and Exu Sete Liras, serving as the counsellor of them both. Holding this function he also ensures the dynamic contrast in this kingdom is upheld, and makes sure that although this is a turbulent and dangerous kingdom, it is at all times kept in a sort of mysterious balance.

You will offer to him seven red peppers filled with meat on a white plate, along with cachaça/aguardiente or rum. White and black candles are good, and tobacco essential, and you can also fumigate his offering with lavender, tobacco and rue, and give him a pipe to stay with him. His *ponto cantado* is as follows:

Boa noite, gente,	Good night people
Boa noite já. (bis)	Good night!
Olha o sapo que pula no chão,	Look the toad jumping on the ground
Andorinha que voa ao luar. (bis)	The swallow that flies to the moon
Salve Exu Malé!	Salutations Exu Malé!
Exu louvei	Exu was singing praises
Exu louvei a encruzilhada	Exu was praising the crossroad
Louvei morada de Exu	Praised the dwelling of Exu
Louvei a rua e a madrugada	Praised the street and the dawn
Sarava Exu Malé	Salutations Exu Malé
E da Calunga	From the Calunga

Approaching Pomba Gira Sete Estrelas
Pomba Gira Seven Stars

SHE IS OF both heaven and ocean, and resonates strongly with the Roma people (ciganos). She is said to take the form of Maria Padilha das Matas (Maria Padilha of the Woods). You will use green and red candles and offer her red wine and absinth on a cloth of night-blue velvet. If you can manage to get fresh leaves

APPENDIX I: APPROACHING THE ENTITY

of datura or brugmansia, use that; you can offer to her shrimps well peppered along with root vegetables, especially manioc, and bean dumplings. She can be approached for inspiration, for deep and marvellous insight and for making people mad with love, with anxiety, with tenderness or whatever you wish, as any emotional realm is within her reach. Her *ponto cantado* is as follows:

Sete Estrelas que brilham no céu	Seven Stars, that shine in the sky
Sete Estrelas que brilham no mar	Seven stars, that shine in the sea
Sete Estrelas que brilham no céu	Seven stars, that shine in the sky
Sete Estrelas que brilham no mar	Seven stars, that shine in the sea
Sete Estrelas que brilham na aruanda	Seven stars that shine in Arruanda
Sete Estrelas que brilham na conga	Seven stars that shine in the shrine
Sete Estrelas que brilham na Inferno	Seven stars that shine in Hell
Sete Estrelas que brilham na gira	Seven stars that shine in the celebration
Ela é a Estrela de Lucifer	She is the star of Lucifer
Que brilham no escuridão	That shines in the darkness
Salve!	Salutations!

Approaching Exu das Cobras
Exu of the Snakes

Approaching the people of the woods, and in particular for gaining the goodwill of Exu das Cobras, you will prepare a dish of manioc flour (rice flour can be used if manioc flour is difficult) that is well mixed with cachaça and freshly ground black peppers and a bit of salt. In this dish place seven eggs. If you want to expand on the offering, add fried chicken to the *padê* along with fresh leaves of medicinal plants or aromatic fresh herbs and plants.

You will in this case also gather flowers, better if you have gathered the flowers yourself in the woods. These can be offered fresh or dry, in the case of the latter you will then offer them on burning coals. Exu das Cobras also likes incense, and in particular myrrh.

You will offer him three candles, one black, one red and one green, and salute the kingdom of the Woods by splashing some cachaça on the floor in front of Exu das Cobras and saying 3 times:

Salve o Reinho das Matas! Salve Exu das Cobras!

Beat your left foot on the floor 3 times, light the candles for Exu das Cobras, and present him with his *padê*, cigars and drinks while singing his *ponto*:

Eu vi o clarão da lua	In the moonlight I saw a glare
Numa brecha na mata escura	A grove in the dark woods
Ouvi barulho de cascavel	I heard the noise of the rattlesnake
Vi a mata se mexendo	Saw the woods moving
E um homem aparecer	And then a man appeared

> *Já era noite, eram altas horas* It was night, it was in the wee hours
> *De joelhos eu louvei meu Mestre* On my knees I was saluting my master
> *Exu das Cobras* Exu of the Snakes

You will sing/recite his *ponto* until you notice his vibration within or without, and will then stay in communion, receptive in the presence of the spirit.

When you want to end the session, thank him for his presence, let the candles burn out by themselves, and the following night take it all to the foot of a tree, to a bush or a crossroad, and dispose of the offerings.

Approaching Exu Tranca Ruas
Exu Roadblocker

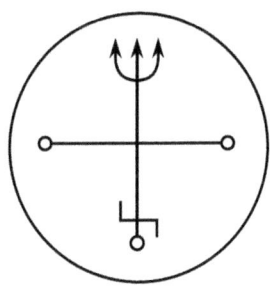

There are several ways of welcoming this Exu to your *firmeza*, and the simple variant is to offer him seven candles in the colours red and black—with a predominance of black—offer up a generous glass of aguardiente, cachaça or whiskey, and sing or play his *pontos* while a cigar, lit and the fumes spreading over his image, is offered up.

As a first encounter, playing recorded *pontos* is perfectly fine. Then you stay in this atmosphere generated by inviting in the spirit. Exu Tranca Ruas is a protective Exu that holds a fair amount of sympathy with the human condition, which makes this Exu a great intercessor. Should a stronger connection be sought, you will make a *padê*, made from flour of some sort heated/boiled with palm oil. In this case you will use manioc, cassava or corn flour, and gather it in a casserole. The measurement would be 500 grams of flour, stirred together with approximately 300 ml of palm oil until the flour turns yellow, and to this you will add peppers—it can be chopped chilli peppers or generous amounts of pepper sauce—and the hotter the better. You will then place these contents in a proper vessel and decorate it with onion rings, preferably red onion, and add to this a haematite and a stone from the street, preferably from as close to your gate/house/apartment as possible, but from the street.

This being done you will trace his *ponto riscado* with chalk on a black cloth and place it in front of him. You will then make popcorn with a very small amount of salt, preferably sea salt, and spread this over the black cloth. You will then place the *padê* on the *ponto* and add a small amount of popcorn to the *padê*. This being done you will make a circle of black and red candles around it and place the statue in front of the *padê*. You will then call him with any of his *pontos*, like for instance the following one:

Deu um clarão na encruzilhada	There was a bright flash in the crossroad
E do clarão surgiu uma gargalhada	and from this a laughter rose
Não era o Sol, não era a Lua	It was not the Sun and it was not the Moon
O que brilhava era o mestre Tranca Ruas	it was the Master Tranca Ruas who was shining

You will offer to him cigar, cachaça, cognac and whiskey, parts are placed in cups and parts are poured over the *padê*. Some of the booze is sprayed over the statue and likewise the cigar fumes are offered to the statue.

Stay with the spirit as the atmosphere is building, partake of the alcohol and cigars—or bring your own cup and cigar—but in moderation, at least at first, because you are aiming at communion and not being overtaken by the spirit. Leave the session with a token of gratitude, respectfully, when you feel the time is right.

Let the candles burn down by themselves, and the day after you will empty the booze in the cups onto the *padê*, but the bottles you keep with the spirit. As night falls, take the *padê* to a crossroad of some form and leave the contents there. No problem in hiding it if this is socially proper where you live. The haematite and street stone you will retrieve and place with him.

Approaching Exu Zé Pelintra

There are several ways of welcoming this Exu to your *firmeza*, and the simple variant is to offer him seven candles in the colours red and white—with a predominance of white—offer up a generous glass of aguardiente, cachaça or whiskey and sing or play his *pontos* while a cigar, lit and the fumes spreading over his image, is offered up.

If you want to go that extra mile and gain further goodwill and benefit from the spirit you will do the following:

You will prepare a drink for him which is composed of lime, cachaça, aguardiente or vodka, and sugar, what is known as caipirinha. The measurement would be more or less a whiskey glass filled one third with booze, three limes cut and squeezed and left inside the glass, and three spoons of sugar; stir and serve in front of him as you offer cigarettes and cigars. You can alternatively give him a glass of cognac mixed with three spoons of good honey. In addition you can also take a mature coconut, remove the top and water from it, and fill this coconut with jerked beef and peppers which you will offer to him along with peanuts and simple sweets on a separate plate.

You will sing his *pontos*, like this one for instance:

Tranca Ruas e Zé pelintra   *Tranca Ruas and Zé Pelintra*
São dois grandes companheiros   *are two great companions*

> *Tranca Ruas na Encruza*   *Tranca Ruas at the crossroad*
> *E Zé Pelintra no terreiro*   *and Zé Pelintra in the Temple*

You will stay with Zé Pelintra and allow the atmosphere to build up, and end it with gratitude when you feel it is proper, allowing the candles to burn down by themselves and disposing of the offerings at a crossroad.

Approaching Pomba Gira da Calunga

You will welcome this powerful force by preparing a dish of unsalted popcorn where you place a piece of pork meat, slightly fried and decorated with roses white, yellow and red, along with a passion fruit or peach. The dish should be generously covered with red peppers along with unscented cigarillos and a bottle of red wine.

You will present her offering on a red cloth where her *ponto* is drawn with black chalk/ink, and in her case the cloth can be the serving vessel itself, no need for a separate vessel for her offering.

You will give her three red candles, two black and two white ones, seven in all.

You will use the following *ponto cantado* for her:

> *Solte os cabelos morena e caia n'água*   Let loose her brown hair and dived into the water
> *Ela é bonita, ela é faceira, é Pomba Gira*   She is beautiful, she is audacious, she is Pomba Gira
> *Mulher de Exu Caveira*   Exu Caveira's woman

APPENDIX I: APPROACHING THE ENTITY

Dentro da Calunga eu vi,   through the calunga I saw
Uma linda mulher gargalhar (bis)   a beautiful woman laughing
Era Pomba Gira da Calunga,   it was Pomba Gira Calunga
Que começava a trabalhar (bis).   That started to work.

This being done you will stay with her and speak from your heart what you desire, and declare appreciation for her arrival to your home.

This being done you will allow the candles to burn down by themselves and take the offering to a cemetery, or to a crossroad as close to the cemetery as possible.

Approaching Pomba Gira Rainha da Calunga

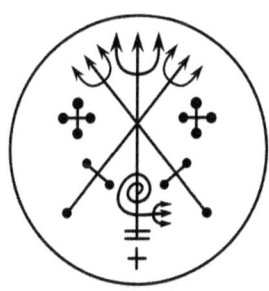

This great Pomba Gira is approached as a Queen of the Cemetery. She is an older and wiser Pomba Gira and so we approach her with some solemnity.

In order to welcome her you will prepare a *padê* consisting of manioc flour, palm oil, oil of sesame seeds and a piquant pepper sauce. The *padê* is decorated with star anise and a yellow candle is placed in its centre, some rings of red onion placed around the candle. Additional candles in red and black are also placed inside the *padê*. Finally a piece of raw pork meat is added to the *padê* together with nine coins.

Prior to approaching her, you will knock three times on the floor with your left hand and say: *Salve Seu Omolu*, and then three more knocks saying: *Salve Exu Veludo*. Offer a cigar—or at least the fumes of a cigar—spray some cachaça on the floor and light one single black candle.

You will then light candles for her, offer her red wine and/or anisette and either cigarillos or strong cigarettes. Draw out her *ponto riscado* and place the *padê* on the *ponto* as you sing her *ponto*.

Leave it overnight, allow the candles to burn out by themselves, and the following night leave the *padê* close to a cemetery, or in a crossroad if proximity to a cemetery is difficult—alternatively it can also be left at the ocean shore or inside the water.

If you want to bring in more of the energy of Calunga, place a thin layer of sea sand in the bottom of the serving vessel together with 9 cowries.

Está na atalaia de Pomba Gira	I am watching out for Pomba Gi
De Pomba Girê para que eu não caia	So She can make sure that I don't fall
Oi Pomba Gire, Pomba Girá oi	Oh Pomba Gira, Pomba Gira Oh!
Oi olha a Pomba Girê, olha a Pomba Girê	Oh look at Pomba Gira, Look at Her
Tem mironga no fundo do mar	She has magic at the bottom of the ocean
No fundo do mar	At the deep of the ocean
Eu via a moça na beira d'água	I saw a girl at the ocean shore
Dentro da Calunga eu vi,	through the calunga I saw
Uma linda mulher gargalhar (bis)	a beautiful woman laughing
Era Pomba Gira da Calunga,	it was Pomba Gira Calunga
Que começava a trabalhar (bis).	That started to work.

Approaching Pomba Gira Maria Mulambo

MARIA MULAMBO IS a central force amongst the legions of Quimbanda known as 'the people of the trash', also known as the *Gangas*, related to the mystery of decay and also finding

APPENDIX I: APPROACHING THE ENTITY

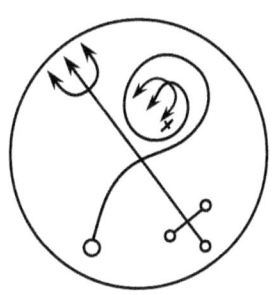

what is precious in unfavourable situations. She can be called upon in all kingdoms and in particular at T-crossroads. Her days are Mondays and Fridays.

In order to welcome her to the *firmeza* you will prepare a *padê* of corn flour fried in palm oil with generous amounts of peppers, placed in a proper serving vessel. To the *padê* is then added sticks of cinnamon, a red lipstick, a bottle of perfume or rosewater, along with seven roses that have been plucked of thorns and tied together with a red ribbon. You will get her a bottle of sparkling white wine/champagne or vermouth, along with scented cigarillos, the better being those scented with cinnamon.

You will light two red candles and one black, and draw her *ponto riscado* with white chalk on red cloth.

You will use the following *pontos cantados* as you present the offerings:

Maria Mulambo da Encruzilhada	Maria Mulambo of the Crossroad
A sua saia é Mulambê...	Your skirt is Mulambé
Ela é Mulambê, Ela é Mulambê.	She is Mulambé.
É hora, é hora, calunga lhe chama,	It is time, it is time, calunga is calling
É hora, é hora Mulambo vai embora. (bis)	It is time for Mulambo to leave
Se pedir que eu mate eu mato,	If you ask me to kill, I will
Se pedir que eu dê eu dô	If you ask me to give pain, I will give pain
Se pedir que eu lhe defenda,	If you ask that I defend
Eu serei seu defensor.	I will be your defender.

As you are singing the *pontos* you will pour the drink over the *padê* and state your request as well as announcing your joy at welcoming her to your home.

In the case of seeking to be reunited with a lost love, you will add to this *padê* an apple cut in two where you add the name of the loved one and your own, each written separately on three pieces of paper. Remove the seed kernel of the apple and place the names inside twisted around one another, stating your wish as you add honey and cinnamon powder to the names, close the apple with a red ribbon, and then place it in the centre of the *padê*.

Let the candles burn out by themselves, and the following night dispose of the *padê* along with the drinks at a T-crossroad.

Approaching Pomba Gira Sete Encruzilhadas
Pomba Gira of the Seven Crossroads

There are several ways of approaching this Pomba Gira, and the simple variant is to offer her seven candles in the colours red and black—with a predominance of red—offer up a generous glass of sparkling wine or whiskey, and sing her *pontos* as a cigarillo (which can be scented with cloves), lit and the fumes spreading over her image, is offered up.

In order to make this entity feel welcome to your life and ritual you will take a red cloth and draw with black chalk on it her *ponto*, and also make a *padê*. The *padê* is made from manioc flour, honey, aromatic (moreso than strong) peppers and a glass of whiskey.

You will then place these contents in a proper vessel and decorate it with onion rings, preferably red onion, and add to the *padê* seven coins or seven cowry shells. You can also sprinkle this with perfume—or even Florida water or rose water. You will place the *padê* on the *ponto* marked on the cloth and make a circle of seven candles, the majority red, which have been tied with a red ribbon. You will then offer up cigarillos, sparkling wine and vermouth, and sing her *pontos*, of which one might be the following:

Pomba Gira na encruzilhada	Pomba Gira at the crossroad
é Pomba Gira de fé	is the Pomba Gira we trust
Mas ela tem uma Rainha	but she has a Queen
que é mulher de Lúcifer	who is the wife of Lucifer
É, é, é mulher,	She is woman
a Quimbanda saúda a Rainha	and Quimbanda salutes the Queen
Pedindo a benção	asking the blessing
pros filhos de fé	for those who put their trust in her

Stay with the spirit as the atmosphere is building, partake of the alcohol and cigars—or bring your own cup and cigar—but in moderation, at least at first, because you are aiming at communion and not being overtaken by the spirit. Leave the session with a token of gratitude, respectfully, when you feel the time is right.

Let the candles burn down by themselves, and the day after you will put the *padê* into the cloth and dispose of it at a crossroad.

p.s. Because the candles are tied with ribbons, please ensure that you do not burn down your house, and take care to secure this in whatever way deemed proper. One option is to make the cloth wet with sparkling wine and water.

APPROACHING POMBA GIRA SETE SAIAS
Pomba Gira of the Seven Skirts

POMBA GIRA SETE Saias is a spirit tied to secrecy, lust, luxury, and the brothel, and is often identified as a gypsy, but this appears to be more by similitude of attitude, and a common reference in the kingdom of the Lyre. Like with the gypsy Pomba Giras, we

find Seven Skirts in all kingdoms and in great variety, hence we find her in the Crossroad, Lyre, Woods and Streets. She is reputed to give excellent counsel and be a great revealer of personal secrets. She is also, like Maria Padilha, reputed to be one of the most powerful forces to sue when it comes to love magic and bindings.

She likes vermouth and champagne, has a preference for deep-fried chicken, and roses should always be present at the *firmeza*.

So, you will welcome her by preparing a *padê* consisting of corn flour that is fried in palm oil. Chopped red onion and generous amounts of red peppers should make part of this mixture. Gather this in a proper vessel, and in the centre you will place three apricots with chicken deep fried in palm oil on top, and present this to her.

You will also get scented cigarillos, sparkling wine and/or vermouth, and seven roses. You will remove the thorns from the roses and tie them up nicely with red and black ribbon. You will use the following *pontos* to greet her:

Pomba Gira Sete Saias	*Pomba Gira of the Seven Skirts*
Mulher de Sete Marido	*Woman of Seven Husbands*
Carrega Sete Navalhas	*who carries Seven Razors*
Na barra do seu vestido	*Hidden in her dress*
Xó, Xó, Xó, Xó	*Xó, Xó, Xó, Xó*
Sete Saias chegou!	*Seven Skirts arrived!*

Approaching Pomba Gira da Praia
Pomba Gira of the Ocean Shore

This Pomba Gira is better approached on a Friday or a Monday, and if it is possible to do so on or close to a full moon it is even better. She is a great force of comfort and solace, but on the other hand she is not only the ease of the ocean shore, but also the cold dark depths, what in Vodou is known as the 'Brijit's of the water', manifesting in the ocean swirls that pull people under with a great and lethal force.

You can offer her a mirror, a lipstick, some jewellery, pearls and sea shells, and similar to be permanently a part of her shrine. These same items can of course also be offered to the ocean itself, or more particularly at the shore. Also, she takes dark blue and white candles, so you can use the colour-scheme of red/blue/white or red/blue/black or blue/black.

You can make a *padê* for her, which will be made from corn or manioc flour and palm oil. But to this you will add shrimps fried in hot peppers and red onion, and coconut meat is added to the *padê*. The *padê* will be decorated with chilli peppers and sea shells, and drenched in vermouth as it is presented to her. A bottle of sparkling wine and aromatic cigarillos are also offered to her with the following *pontos*:

Pomba Gira da Praia,	Pomba Gira of the ocean shore
É uma linda Mulher,	She is a beautiful woman
Ela é bonita,	she is astonishing
Ela gosta do prazer.	She adores pleasure

Oi kererê, kererê,	*oi kererê, kererê*
Pomba Gira da Praia,	*Pomba Gira of the Ocean Shore*
No meio da Areia,	*In the middle of the sand*
No meio da Praia.	*In the middle of the beach*

The *padê* is better disposed of at the ocean shore the night after, but if this is not possible, any crossroad somewhat connected to vibrant nightlife will do.

Appendix II
The Kingdoms of Quimbanda

THE CONCEPT OF kingdoms in Quimbanda is commonly said to be mirrored by the organization of tribal nations in Kongo, where within given districts we find several smaller units or villages, each with their kings. But the notion of kingdoms might also owe its influence in Quimbanda partly to the cults of Jurema and Catimbó in the north-east of Brazil where Zé Pelintra is considered to be a master of the art of Jurema, whilst also exercising a domineering influence over the people of the street in Quimbanda. Central in Catimbó and Jurema is the existence of various kingdoms, each of these realms inhabited by a master that teaches quite particular mysteries of magic and healing. This concept was introduced in Quimbanda by Mãe Ieda de Ogum in 1962 through her work with Exu Rei das Sete Encruzilhadas, commonly called Seu Sete, or Mr. Seven, that led to a very interesting form of Quimbanda in the south of Brazil under the denomination Quimbanda de Cruzeiro e Almas or Quimbanda Gaúcha.

The organization of Exus into kingdoms derived in turn from the various attempts to systematize the various Exus into lineages in the works of Leal de Souza in 1925, Lourenço Braga in 1941, and Aluizio Fontenelle in 1950, a way of making sense of the essential vibrations of Exu and understanding what sort of power or energy a given Exu would have access to. In extension, this also means that when speaking of 'going to the kingdom', or if someone has an affinity with a specific kingdom, this means that this particular place holds a power that is more accessible for a person presenting a similar vibration. For instance a person that holds an affinity with the kingdom of the Crossroad and the Woods will, in the crossroad of the woods, ruled by Exu Tiriri, have access to a very precise power and force, but will also have a natural connection with Exus of the Woods and the Crossroads in general. As we see, in the organization of Exus in the kingdoms we also find a sub-organization into particular places within a kingdom where a specific Exu is the boss, in the sense of this given vibration being stronger, as in the example with Exu Tiriri, who is an Exu of the kingdom of the Crossroads, but his power is even more tangible in a crossroad found in the woods. Further, this means that it is possible to go to these exact locations in the world with a candle, a cigarette and a glass of cachaça to get in touch with a very specific manifestation of Exu.

The kingdoms also present the Exus and Pomba Giras in their original station, as guardian spirits of specific places of power in nature and the world. In the kingdoms we meet original powers, whilst in the lines we meet teaching spirits. To have a good idea about the kingdoms is most useful, because no work is being done unless licence is granted from the kingdom we work with. Exus from other lines and kingdoms can then enter as parts of the spirit host when a particular work is done, depending on what kind of work is done in the particular kingdom. Just like an army distributes its soldiers and commanders depending on the type of expedition being made, so it is with the spirit host established in kingdoms, workings, and in life.

The seven kingdoms with their king and queen are as follows:

1. The kingdom of the Crossroads (Reino das Encruzilhadas) is under the command of Exu King of the Seven Crossroads (Exu Rei das Sete Encruzilhadas) and Pomba Gira Queen of the Seven Crossroads (Pomba Gira Rainha das Sete Encruzilhadas). This kingdom concerns everything related to where the visible and invisible worlds cross or interact, and as such the mysteries of possession, mediumship and spirit interaction belong to this kingdom. Naturally any and every physical crossroad also belongs to this kingdom. The crossroads shape be in the format of a T, X or +, but also in this kingdom we have the idea of a crossroad being a place where powers converge.

2. The kingdom of the Crossing or Big Cross (Reino dos Cruzeiros) is commanded by Exu King of the Seven Crossings (Exu Rei dos Sete Cruzeiros) and Pomba Gira Queen of the Seven Crossings (Pombagira Rainha dos Sete Cruzeiros). This kingdom is clearly the most mysterious one, as the Cruzeiro spoken about here is the large cross in the centre of a Catholic graveyard, where candles are lit to one's ancestors and patron saints. The Cruzeiro is seen as the place where the souls are returning to the invisible realms under the shelter of divine protection and observance. Hence in this kingdom we find much wisdom about the invisible realm in regard to what we might call transmigration and transubstantiation, and so the Cruzeiro represents a quite categorical mystery, similar to Crossroads, but within a very distinct design.

3. The kingdom of the Woods (Reino das Matas) is commanded by Exu King of the Woods (Exu Rei das Matas) and Pomba Gira Queen of the Woods (Pombagira Rainha das Matas). This kingdom is the original kingdom, as the Exus of the woods represent the source for the other kingdoms. It was here in the woods that powers were first established and from there spread out over the world.

4. The kingdom of the Small Calunga (Reino da Calunga Pequena) is the name given to the Cemetery. This kingdom is commanded by Exu king of the Seven Calungas (Exu Rei das Sete Calungas) and Pomba Gira Queen of the Seven Calungas (Pombagira Rainha das Sete Calungas). This kingdom is naturally tied in to the mysteries of the graveyard and to the communion with the other side in a general and overarching way, whilst the next kingdom, the kingdom of Souls, concerns itself with the peculiarities and singularities of the mysteries of death.

5. The kingdom of the Souls (Reino das Almas) is under the command of Exu Omulu, also known as King of Souls (Exu Rei das Almas), and Pomba Gira Queen of Souls (Pombagira Rainha das Almas). This kingdom preserves the memory of Quimbanda originally being established through the cunning of the *pretos-velhos* or 'Old Blacks' from Congo and Cabinda that ensured the legacy we today understand to be Quimbanda. This kingdom is also known as the kingdom of mounds, in the first instance a reference to the mound as a burial site and a doorway to the invisible, but also in relation to specific points where souls leave their earthly existence, like morgues, hospitals, sites of accidental death and so forth.

6. The kingdom of the Harp or Lira (Reino da Lira) is commanded by Exu Lucifer and Pomba Gira Maria Padilha. In some traditions of Quimbanda, Exu Lucifer is equal to Exu Rei das Sete Liras (Exu King of the Seven Harps) and Maria Padilha is in reference to this kingdom also known as Queen of Candomblé and Queen of all 'Marys', in the sense of Mary as a denomination for all Pomba Giras. Even if some practitioners have suggested that the name of the kingdom is a memory of the city of Lira in present-day Uganda, it still remains that the harp as a musical instrument is what has become associated with this kingdom that contains all the powers we find in the nightlife, the taverns and the bohemian spirit. The harp might seem a dull instrument to give to this kingdom that trembles with music, poetry, raves, music and the criminal underworld, but the harp was the instrument of the biblical king David, a hedonist and murderous poet in his own right.

7. The kingdom of the Ocean Shore (Reino da Praia) is commanded by Exu King of the Ocean shore (Exu Rei da Praia/Exu Gererê) and Pomba Gira Queen of the

Ocean shore (Rainha da Praia). This is a very mysterious kingdom, as it is also the kingdom of the Calunga Grande, the Great Cemetery, that is also the entrance to the invisible world, the realm of ancestors and spirits of wisdom. The ocean shore itself is a place of healing, inspiration and repose, but the shore also gives us access to the ocean itself with its undines and marine ghosts and legends.

Breaking down the kingdoms further, we have also nine *povos*, or peoples, we can translate as 'crews', 'clans' or 'hordes' that have an Exu as their commander. This gives us a total of 63 *povo de Exu*, which of course is more a symbolic number, than real calculus. Let us take the kingdom of Crossroads as an example of how this looks like.

KINGDOM OF THE CROSSROADS

1) The Crew of the Crossroad of the Street – Exu Tranca-Ruas (Roadblocker)
2) The Crew of the Crossroad of the Lyre – Exu Sete Encruzilhadas (Seven Crossroads)
3) The Crew of the Crossroad of the Mound – Exu das Almas (Exu of the Souls)
4) The Crew of the Crossroad of the Trails – Exu Marabô
5) The Crew of the Crossroad of the Woods – Exu Tiriri
6) The Crew of the Crossroad of the Calunga – Exu Veludo (Mr. Velvet)
7) The Crew of the Crossroad of the Square – Exu Morcego (Mr. Bat)
8) The Crew of the Crossroad of the Ambient/Room – Exu Sete Gargalhadas (Seven Laughters)
9) The Crew of the Crossroad of the Ocean shore – Exu Mirim (Exu 'Shorty')

What is important to take note of is that when we break down the kingdoms into smaller segments, we can see how the idea of crossroads as places of power is central in Quimbanda and how these particular crossroads of powers are inhabited by a very distinct group of spirits that is in league with an Exu. For instance, Exu Tranca-Ruas being the chief of the crossroads we meet in the streets crossing and overlapping is easy to understand, but what about the crossroad of the town square, how should we understand this particular crossroad or crossroads? These crossroads, like the crossroads of the lyre and the ambient/room, are points of power that are generated by momentous actions and meetings, hence they are not necessarily permanent. Let's take two examples. Two people involved in some sort of clandestine or criminal activity can generate a temporary crossroad of power in this kingdom, resorting to the powers of this particular crew that takes their powers from the Square.

In the same vein a bench in the square that received the energetic charge of lovers in heat, the secret words of commitment or the blood given to the bench by a murderer, will generate a permanent crossroad in the shape of a bench. This also means that someone with a strong connection with Exu Veludo will also have an affinity with the Calunga, the Cemetery and the Ocean depth, which are the places where someone working with Veludo will have greater success in obtaining results, and will also be places that enhance the practitioner's natural power or *força*. But it doesn't stop there, because we also have paths or qualities of the Exus and Pomba Giras. Let us use Exu Veludo and Exu Meia-Noite (Mr. Midnight) as examples.

Exu Veludo is an Exu with strong ties to Arabic parts of Africa, and his name in Quimbanda of Mr. Velvet is due to his taste for finer things, jewellery, decorated daggers and other weaponry. He can appear similar to a prince from the *Arabian Nights* just as he can appear as a well-dressed gentleman. This variable form of manifestation is caused by Exu Veludo being the name of a legion of Exus, all of them with similar yet distinct histories that explain how they became Exus and why their chosen

APPENDIX II: THE KINGDOMS OF QUIMBANDA

form was taken. He is an Exu well-versed in dismantling malefic workings, clearing paths, and all forms of cemetery workings. All these facets find resonance in one of his qualities or paths, some of which are as follows:

Exu Veludo da Meia-Noite
(*Mr. Velvet of the Midnight*)
Exu Veludo Cigano
(*Mr. Velvet the Gypsy*)
Exu Veludo 7 Encruzilhadas
(*Mr. Velvet of the 7 Crossroads*)
Exu Veludo Menino (Veludinho)
(*Little Velvet*)
Exu Veludo dos 7 Cruzeiros
(*Mr. Velvet of the 7 Cruzeiros*)
Exu Veludo das Almas
(*Mr. Velvet of the Souls*)
Exu Veludo dos Infernos
(*Mr. Velvet of the Many Hells*)
Exu Veludo da Calunga
(*Mr. Velvet of the Cemetery*)
Exu Veludo da Praia
(*Mr. Velvet of the Ocean Shore*)
Exu Veludo do Oriente
(*Mr. Velvet of the Orient*)
Exu Veludo Sigatana
(*Mr. Velvet Sigatana*: an Angolan crossroad spirit whose name in Kikongo means 'sorcerer who lives at the bottom of the river')
Exu Veludo do Lixo
(*Mr. Velvet of the Garbage*)

When we look at Exu Meia-Noite, Mr. Midnight, we find a different set of qualities due to his Kongolese origin and strong ties to Brazil, especially the state of Minas Gerais, and his mastery over sorcery and astrology. This complex of factors also gives way for many Exus in this legion preferring the form of the heretic priest, expanding on its own mysterious Kongolese Christianity of whose qualities we find the following:

> Exu Meia-Noite da Calunga
> (*Mr. Midnight of the Cemetery*)
> Exu Meia-Noite das Almas
> (*Mr. Midnight of the Souls*)
> Exu Meia-Noite da Praia
> (*Mr. Midnight of the Ocean Shore*)
> Exu Meia-Noite do Mar
> (*Mr. Midnight of the Sea*)
> Exu Meia-Noite do Oriente
> (*Mr. Midnight of the Orient*)
> Exu Meia-Noite das 7 Encruzilhadas
> (*Mr. Midnight of the 7 Crossroads*)
> Exu Meia-Noite da Capela
> (*Mr. Midnight of the Chapel*)
> Exu Meia-Noite do Cruzeiro
> (*Mr. Midnight of the Cruzeiro*)
> Exu Meia-Noite da Mata
> (*Mr. Midnight of the Woods*)

This way of cataloguing and understanding a prime force and its manifestation in other places would inform us about the many and versatile places we can find a specific Exu, and in the same way the person that is working with, let's say, Mr. Midnight will have, in theory, access to these various places of power and qualities, as Mr. Midnight, wanting to work with a particular human, might seek to establish this relationship because it is in harmony with one specific quality or path.

Bibliography

Acher, Frater & Sabogal, José Gabriel. *Clavis Goêtica*. Hadean Press. 2021

Alkmin, Zaydan. *Zé Pelintra; Dono da Noite, Rei da Magia*. Pallas Editora. 2004

Alva, Antônio. *Trabalhos Práticos de Magia-Negra*. Pallas. 1985

Bastide, Roger. *As Religiões Africanas no Brasil*. Pioneira. 1960

Braga, Lourenço. *Umbanda, magia branca e Quimbanda, magia negra*. Editor Borsoi. 1942

Carneiro, Edison. *Religiões Negras*. Civilização Brasileira. 1936

Cintra, Raimundo. *Candomblé e Umbanda*. Edições Paulinas. 1985

Fontenelle, Aluizio. *A Umbanda Através dos Séculos*. Espiritualista. 1950

Fontenelle, Aluizio. *Exu*. Espiritualista. 1951

Fu-Kiau, Kimbwandende Kia Bunseki. *African Cosmology of the Bântu-Kôngo*. Athelia Henrietta Press. 1980

Isaia, Artur Cesar & Manoel, Ivan Aparecido (eds.). *Espiritismo & Religiões Afro-Brasileiras*. Editora Unesp. 2011

Maggi, Humberto & Rivas, Veronica. *Maria Padilla: Queen of the Souls*. Hadean Press. 2015

Mendonça, Evandro. *Rituais de Quimbanda*. Anubis. 2016

Parés, Luis Nicolau. *A Formação de Candomblé*. Editora Unicamp. 2018

Ramos, Arthur. *O Negro Brasileiro*. Companhia Editora Nacional. 1940

Rodrigues, Nina. *Os Africanos no Brasil*. Companhia Editora Nacional. 1945

Sampaio, Gabriela dos Reis. *A História do Feiticeiro Juca Rosa*. Ph.D dissertation. Unicamp. 2000

Da Silva, Vagner Gonçalves. *Candomblé e Umbanda*. Editora Atica. 1994

De Souza, Leal. *O Espiritismo – a magia e as Sete Linhas de Umbanda*. Editora Arruanda. 2019

Tausiet, María. 'The Guardian of Hell: Popular Demonology,

Exorcism and Mysticism in Baroque Spain'. In Goodare, Julian et. al. (eds.), *Demonology and Witch-hunting in Early Modern Europe.* Routledge. 2020

Trindade, Diamantino. *A Construção Histórica da Literatura Umbandista.* Conhecimento Editorial. 2010

Trindade, Liana. *Exu. Poder e Perigo.* Icone Editora. 1985

Valente, Waldemar. *Sincretismo Religioso Afro-Brasileiro*, Companhia Editora Nacional, 1977

Wilbert, Johannes. 'The Order of Dark Shamans among the Warao'. In Whitehead, N.L. & White, R (eds.), *In Darkness and Secrecy.* Duke University Press. 2004

Index

A

abolition (of slavery) 7
alcohol 4, 25, 33, 75, 79, 80, 155
alumbrados 82-83
amaci. See magic, baths
amulet. *See patuá*
ancestors 24, 39, 62, 67-68, 159
  shrine for 63-64
ancestral line 30
àsé 75
Astaroth 40, 43, 86
  as Pomba Gira 38
assentamento 28, 29, 44, 99, 145, 146, 149, 150
auto da fé 82

B

Bantu
  and Exu 56
  language 76
  Quimbanda in 15-16
  spirit pots 149-150
  structure of ritual 24
  treatment of women 84
beatas 82
Belzebub 38, 40, 41, 43, 55
benzedeiras 67, 137, 138
Braga, Lourenço 5

C

caboclos 11, 20, 26, 47-48, 49, 50, 76
  of waters 11

cabula
  as place 20, 27, 37, 39, 44, 98-99, 100
  as practice 90-93, 161
Candomblé 7-10, 17-18, 20, 30, 45-46
crossroad 12, 39, 49, 51-52, 53, 54-55, 56-58, 59, 81, 89, 95, 152-153, 159-160
crowned 43, 76-77, 79
curandeirismo 90

D

de Souza, Leal 3, 5, 10, 13
Devil, the 5, 33, 34, 36, 53, 55, 90, 135, 147, 152, 153
Dikenga. *See* Yowa cosmogram
do Rio, João 17, 18, 90, 91

E

Encruzilhada. See crossroad
entheogens 92
eros 83, 115, 119
Èsú 53, 55, 74, 75, 76
  feeding 54
Exu
  amorality of 31, 48, 49, 50, 76, 77, 78, 80, 106, 162
  as Devil 34
  as guardian spirit 31
  fusion of Exu, Èsú and Devil 53–54
  'having Exu' 28-30
  house of. *See tronco*
  imposter 124, 128
  incarnations of 71-72, 77, 153
  nature of 56

F

fascination 116, 135, 136
Fates, the 122
figa 138

INDEX

firmeza 65, 96, 97, 98, 108, 138
Friday 70, 131, 167, 185
fumigations 142

G

grimoires 12, 41, 89
Grimorium Verum 40, 55, 88, 93

H

hustling, hustlers 22, 34, 37, 71-72, 147

I

Ifá 13, 41, 54, 74, 91
initiation 30, 92

J

Jupiter 70

K

King of Quimbanda. *See* Lucifer
kingdoms. *See* Quimbanda, kingdoms of
kisimbi 81, 158, 159
kiumba 59
Kongo 45
  and Exu 76
  cosmology 67
  spirit pots 149-150
  worldview 26-27

L

lineage 29, 58
Litanies of Satan 35–36
Lucifer 38, 40, 43, 45, 55, 56, 74
  Exu 78
lucky dime 129

M
macumba 5, 9-10, 11-12, 17-19, 21, 23-24, 45, 61-62, 84
Maggi, Humberto 5, 6
magic 70, 109
  attacks 123-124
  baths 9, 128, 136, 141
  black 5-6, 30, 88-89, 105
  chimerical 110
  contagious 129
  folk 46, 67, 83, 90, 117, 140
  nefarious 110, 111, 136
  organic material used in 117
  placebo 110, 112
  sympathetic 140
Maioral 38, 40, 41, 42, 43, 55, 56, 98, 99, 103
  emissaries of 41
  seal of 42
malandragem 73, 75. *See also* hustling, hustlers
maleficia 121, 124, 136
Mass of the Dead 121
Mbumba Nzila. *See* Pomba Gira
mediumship 43, 63, 65, 66, 77
Monday 70, 125

N
native (indigenous) spirits. *See caboclos*
Nganga 68
nigromancia 89
nkisi 26, 32, 34, 36, 46, 68, 146, 150, 161, 162
Nkosi 51

O
Obaluwaye. *See* Omolu
ocean 68, 94, 158-159
offerings 25, 64, 106–108, 130-132
Ogum 11, 41, 50, 51, 54-55

INDEX

manifestations of 15
Old Blacks 5, 11, 20, 23, 90, 142
Omolu 11-12, 14, 99, 101, 125, 127
oracles 155-157
Orixás 10, 12-13, 21, 31, 46, 51, 75, 92
  as devils 55

P

pact 15, 30, 34, 110-112, 127, 145, 153, 161
Padilha, Maria 81, 83, 95
Padilla, Maria 81-82
Pambujila. *See* Pomba Gira
patuá 129, 130, 131, 171
planets, seven traditional 70
Pomba Gira 12, 13-14, 16, 28, 30, 35, 41, 43, 48-51, 53, 56, 58,
    59, 65-66, 70, 79, 93-94, 98-99, 109, 115, 147, 148-150
  as a literary theme 84
  do Inferno 38, 40, 41, 86
  incarnations of 71-72, 77, 153
  nature of 56
  varieties of 84–85
poppet 115, 124, 126
possession 24, 57, 109
  two-headed 66
pretos-velhos. *See* Old Blacks
protection vessel 138

Q

Quimbanda
  Angolan heritage 10, 26
  as 'left side' of Umbanda 25-26
  Bantu heritage 10, 26, 69
  chain of command 40-41
  code of honour 79, 80, 87
  essence of 89
  King of. *See* Lucifer, Exu

kingdoms of 14, 16, 25, 39, 58-59, 133
Kongo heritage 9-11
lines of 11-13
Queen of. *See* Maria Padilha
seven lines of 11–13
world view 94

R

Ramos, Arthur 9, 10, 24, 150, 195
Rodrigues, Nina 9, 91, 195
Rosa, Juca 22, 23, 24, 25, 27, 195

S

saints 11, 25, 46, 69-71, 91
  Saint Anthony 20, 50
  Saint Cyprian 12, 20
  Saint Expedite 161
  Saint Lazarus 12, 20, 161, 162
  Saint Michael 41, 42, 43, 69, 100
Satanism 31, 32, 34, 69
Saturday 70, 126, 167
Saturn 60, 80, 93, 94, 126, 155
shrine. *See firmeza*
Spirit House. *See assentamento*
Spiritism 45, 88
  'low' 61-63
  'high' 62

Sunday 70, 125
Sun, the 4, 19, 41, 67, 68, 69, 102, 154, 176

T

temple. *See cabula, tronco*
Thursday 70
tobacco 51, 54, 65, 93, 106, 109, 153-155
trident 4, 14

INDEX

tronco 39, 43-44, 99-101, 136
Tuesday 70, 126

U

Umbanda 15, 18-20, 23, 30, 43, 62-63, 92, 140, 160-161

V

Venus 11, 93, 94, 117, 118
Vodou 8, 20, 159

W

Wednesday 70

X

Xangô 11, 45, 46
  line of 47

Y

Yoruba 8, 10, 21, 24, 51, 58, 76
Yowa cosmogram 67

Z

Zélio, Fernandino de Morais 18, 19, 20, 25, 26, 62, 72, 140
Zé Pelintra 21, 22, 73, 77, 130, 132, 147-148

www.ingramcontent.com/pod-product-compliance
Lightning Source LLC
Chambersburg PA
CBHW070648160426
43194CB00009B/1623